THE ASCENT
OF NANDA DEVI

H. W. TILMAN

The shrine of the goddess:
First view of the mountain from Rishi valley

THE ASCENT
OF NANDA DEVI

H. W. TILMAN

TILMAN

First published 1937 by Cambridge University Press
This edition published 2015 by Tilman Books
www.tilmanbooks.com
a joint venture by
Lodestar Books www.lodestarbooks.com
and Vertebrate Publishing www.v-publishing.co.uk

Cover design by Jane Beagley
Vertebrate Graphics Ltd. www.v-graphics.co.uk

Lodestar Books has asserted its right
to be identified as the Editor of this Work

Series editor Dick Wynne
Series researcher Bob Comlay

The publisher has made reasonable effort to locate
the holders of copyright in the illustrations in this book,
and will be pleased to hear from them regarding
correct attribution in future editions

A CIP catalogue record for this book
is available from the British Library

ISBN 978-1-909461-18-5

Typeset in Baskerville from Storm Type Foundry
Printed and bound by Pulsio, Bulgaria
All papers used by Tilman Books are sourced responsibly

FSC
www.fsc.org
FSC-C095224

Contents

Photographs

Maps

Foreword

John Porter

I FIRST READ THE ASCENT OF NANDA DEVI as a teenager in high school. It was one of those books that fired my urge to climb, and to find a way to create my own adventures, such was the power of the storytelling and the enormity of the feat achieved by that small Anglo-American party in 1936. The first ascent of Nanda remains one of the greatest mountaineering achievements of all time. The 1936 party was a small but strong team of seven climbers supporting each other with carries high on the mountain after their small band of Sherpa became ill. Despite illness in their own team, Tilman and Odell reached the summit after many weeks, overcoming difficulties at the extreme edge of their experience. The fact that the mountain was climbed during the monsoon storms makes it even more remarkable. And true to the exploring spirit of the day, the expedition came out of the Nanda Devi Sanctuary by a completely unknown route.

In the eighty years since the ascent, there have been many better known 'Himalayan breakthroughs', such as the first ascents of Annapurna and Everest, the South Face of Annapurna, and increasingly during the 70s and 80s, bold, lightweight ascents of very difficult routes alpine-style, such as the Scott, Boardman and Tasker route of Kangchenjunga and most recently, Ueli Steck's solo ascent of the South Face of Annapurna. But what makes the 1936 ascent totally unique is the totality of the achievement. It was so much more than just a story of getting to the summit of a big unclimbed peak.

At 7816m (25,643ft), Nanda Devi is not only the highest mountain entirely within India, it is also one of the most sacred and beautiful. It is remarkably steep on all sides, rising 3300m from is base both from the north and south, making its profile of steepness similar to that of K2. But getting in to K2 is easy compared to getting to the bottom of

Nanda Devi. The peak is defended on all sides by rings of mountains of between 6000–7000m. It took nearly fifty years for explorers to force a way into this sanctuary. After three failures to penetrate the mountain's defences, one of the early pioneers, Hugh Ruttledge, described the attempt to reach the sanctuary as more difficult than going to the North Pole. Success in reaching the beautiful inner sanctuary of meadows, lakes and glaciers was achieved finally in 1934 by Tilman himself with his good friend Eric Shipton. They forced a route up the 10-mile long Rishi Ganga which involved some difficult rock climbing.

Himalayan climbing was still in its infancy in 1936. Climbers had been higher on the north side of Everest and on Kangchenjunga, but no one had climbed such a difficult and dangerous mountain. The way climbers recorded their achievements and their relationship with nature was very different from today. Failure was more common than success and was seen as potentially more fulfilling. As Tilman writes: 'The splendour of the mountain is undimmed or even enhanced, and the writer can be trusted to see to it that the honour of man is, at the lowest, not diminished.' The journey was always more important than the arrival, and it is the descriptions of the journey as much as the climb that make this an enthralling book.

Going back to read the book again after more than 50 years, what struck me was the richness and thoroughness of the writing, the use of wry humour and modesty in the telling of every aspect of the adventure. The starting point for Tilman's style is reverence, reverence for the mountains, the people, the culture and religion and for the pioneers who came before. The opening chapters help explain why Garhwal is felt by many to be the most beautiful region of the Himalaya, and how the Goddess Nanda took sanctuary on the summit of the mountain to avoid being ravished by her father's murderer. Ironically, Tom Longstaff, who wrote the original foreword, and had himself failed to penetrate into the sanctuary, wrote: 'climbing this peak would be a sacrilege too horrible to contemplate.' But it was to Longstaff that Tilman offered the chance to write that foreword. Longstaff accepted because despite his earlier doubt, 'news of success filled me with delight. A laconic telegram reached me in Shetland: "two reached the top August 29": no names. They had deserved the honour: here was humility not pride, and gratitude for a permitted experience.'

The first plate in the book shows a porter standing on the gateway to 'the shrine of the goddess' with Nanda Devi behind. This was taken very near the spot where our small 1978 Changabang expedition shared a camp with our porters. I can imagine the porters with Tilman clapping, dancing and singing the night away as ours did 42 years later. They were in the presence of their goddess. When reading Tilman, we find the same sense of reverence.

Foreword to the First Edition

T. G. Longstaff

IN THE OPINION OF COMPETENT JUDGES the achievement narrated in the following pages is the finest mountain ascent yet made, either in the Himalaya or anywhere else. It so happens that, besides being very difficult, Nanda Devi is also the highest mountain that has yet been climbed to the top.

This is the story of a self-sufficing party of friends who provided their own finance and eschewed publicity. Professor Graham Brown, of Mount Foraker fame, was the connecting link between the English and American mountaineers. There was no official leader: but when the moment came for the final attempt on the peak the author of this book was voted into the lead to direct the activities of the whole team. Significantly enough Tilman did not give himself a place in the first party; it was only the unfortunate and accidental illness of Houston which made him Odell's companion on the successful climb. Mountaineers will regret that the chances of the weather prevented others from attaining the summit. But owing to the collapse of the Sherpa porters, and the consequent necessity for the party to carry its own camps up the mountain, this was even more of a 'team success' than most high climbs have been. Every single member shares the honours of this great climb.

Double crowned Ushba in the central Caucasus is the only mountain which I can compare for beauty with Nanda Devi. But the surroundings of the latter are more beautiful even than in Svanetia. Nanda Devi was my goal years before I set foot in the Himalaya. After six visits to the Snows I still believe that Garhwal is the most beautiful country of all High Asia. Neither the primitive immensity of the Karakorum, the aloof domination of Mount Everest, the softer Caucasian beauties of the Hindu Kush, nor any of the many other regions of Himachal can compare with Garhwal. Mountain and valley, forest and alp, birds and animals, butterflies and flowers all combine to make a sum of delight unsurpassed elsewhere. The human interest is stronger than in any other mountain region of the world, for these anciently named peaks are written of in the earliest annals of the Indo-Aryan race. They are the home of the Gods. For two hundred million Hindus the shrines of Garhwal still secure supreme merit to the devout pilgrim.

The prettiest compliment I have ever received was Tilman's request that I should write a foreword for his book. He knows that I have always believed that Nanda Devi reigned over the most supremely beautiful part of all Himalaya: that only three years ago, in the 'Mountaineering' volume of the Lonsdale Series, I had written that the climbing of this peak would be a sacrilege too horrible to contemplate. I was thinking of the probable self-glorification of man in a 'conquest' over Nature at her sublimest, and of the loss of one more mystery. Yet in the event news of success filled me with delight. A laconic telegram reached me in Shetland: 'two reached the top August 29': no names. They had deserved the honour: here was humility not pride, and gratitude for a permitted experience.

Author's Preface

A PROPOS OF WRITING BOOKS Dr Johnson's opinion was that 'any block-head can write if he sets himself doggedly to it'. I should like to alter that and say, 'any blockhead can write a book if he has something to write about'— that I have anything to write about is entirely due to my companions, British and American, to whom I dedicate this book.

The thanks of the whole party are due to Mrs A. E. Browne of Ranikhet for much help and hospitality, and to Messrs E. O. Shebbeare and F. W. Champion for assistance in India.

I have to acknowledge my indebtedness for many facts about Garhwal and Almora to the *District Gazetteers of the United Provinces* by Mr H. G. Walton, and to Mr A. H. Mumm's *Five Months in the Himalaya* for some of the climbing history.

My thanks are due to all those members of the party who generously put their photographs at my disposal: to *The Times* for permission to republish those opposite pages 10 and 104*, and to the *New York Times* for allowing me to use again those facing pages 24, 162, 180†.

H.W.T.
Seacroft
Wallasey
March 1937

---

*   Photos 3 and 15 in this edition
†   Photos 5, 29, 30, 34 in this edition

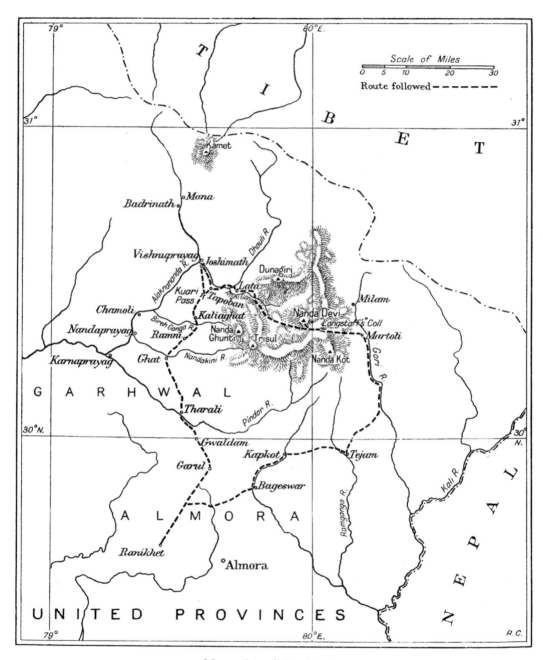

Map 1: Expedition Route

CHAPTER I

MYTHOLOGICAL
AND GEOGRAPHICAL

IT IS QUESTIONABLE whether the story of a successful attempt on a new peak will be as acceptable as a story of failure; at any rate to lovers of mountains or to those who know one end of an ice-axe from the other. These will perhaps be more inclined to echo the words of David's lament and cry, 'Tell it not in Gath, publish it not in the streets of Askelon.'

If an account of the climbing of Everest is ever written, I take leave to doubt whether it will be as widely read as have been the stories of successive failures. For, say what one may, when the summit is reached some of the mystery and grandeur surrounding a peak hitherto untrodden by man is lost; and a book recounting the fall of one of the giants will be bought—or by mountaineers more likely borrowed—with misgiving and read with loathing. But so complex is our make-up that the pleasure which success brings far outweighs any remorseful pangs, and friends, even mountaineering friends, congratulate the triumphant party sincerely instead of damning them heartily. And, as if that was not enough, pressure of various kinds results in the members of the expedition putting on record their experiences so that all may profit by them, and the invincibility of yet another great mountain is thereby imperilled. Perhaps when the millennium dawns, of the writing of books there will be an end, at least of mountaineering books; if there are then any unconquered peaks remaining, come what may, successive generations will think them still unconquered to the end of time.

Stories of unsuccessful climbs are in a different category. The splendour of the mountain is undimmed or even enhanced, and the writer can be trusted to see to it that the honour of man is, at the lowest, not diminished. But having now hinted at the motives impelling the writing of this account it is time to cut the cackle and come to the 'osses; for it would puzzle a conjuror to explain satisfactorily a habit (not confined to mountaineers) of believing one thing and doing another.

Before leaving for the Himalaya in May, I was asked by an otherwise intelligent man whether it would be summer or winter out there when we arrived. This is mentioned in no critical spirit, but only to show that what one man assumes to be common knowledge may be known only to very few. A banker, for instance, popularly supposed to be without a soul, may know nothing and care less about mountains, but be deeply interested in music or literature; and, conversely, mountaineers may not know the most elementary principles of banking or, possibly, grammar.

To some the Himalaya may be only a name vaguely associated perhaps with a mountain called Everest: to geologists they provide a vast field for the starting and running of new hares; to other learned men, glaciologists, ethnologists, or geographers, the Himalaya are a fruitful source of debate in which there is no common ground, not even the pronunciation of the name; while to the mountaineer they furnish fresh evidence, if such were needed, of the wise dispensation of a bountiful Providence. For, lo, when the Alps are becoming too crowded, not only with human beings but with huts, the Himalaya offer themselves to the more fanatical devotee—a range fifteen hundred miles long, containing many hundred of peaks, nearly all unclimbed, and all of them so much higher than the Alps that a new factor of altitude has to be added to the usual sum of difficulties to be overcome; and withal to be approached through country of great loveliness, inhabited by peoples who are always interesting and sometimes charming. Here seemingly is a whole new world to conquer, but it is a world which man with his usual perversity, flying in the face of Providence, has reduced to comparatively small dimensions: for what with political boundaries, restrictions, and jealousies, the accessible area is less than one-third of the whole. And though European travellers and climbers may grouse about this state of affairs, Europeans are, I suppose, largely to blame. For with the present state of the outside world before their eyes the rulers of Tibet, Nepal, and Bhutan can scarcely be blamed, and might well be praised, for wishing their own people to have as little as possible to do with ourselves.

Main Peak   East Peak

Peaks of Nanda Devi from N.E. shoulder of Nanda Kot
Photograph by Dr T. G. Longstaff, June 11th 1905

Sikkim, Kashmir, and Garhwal remain open to travellers, though the first two are not without their restrictions; restrictions which we were to experience. Garhwal is a small district almost in the centre of the Himalayan chain and lying about two hundred miles north-east of Delhi. It is divided into British Garhwal and the native state of Tehri Garhwal, but here we need trouble ourselves only with the first, which did not come under British control until after the Nepalese War of 1815. Originally the country was in the hands of a number of petty chieftains, each with his own fortress or castle; the word 'garh' itself means a castle. In the early years of the nineteenth century it was overrun by the Ghurkas, who, not content with this acquisition, extended their ravages down to the plains and thus came into collision with the ruling Power and brought about the Nepalese War. In the early stages of the war we reaped our usual crop of defeats and disasters, but in the end (and up to the present this also has been usual) we muddled through and drove the Ghurkas back within their present boundaries; and, as a slight reward for the trouble to which we had been put, we annexed the greater part of Garhwal for ourselves. It is roughly rectangular, about a hundred miles from north to south and fifty from east to west, and diagonally across the northern half runs the Himalayan chain. In this short section of the range there are two peaks over 25,000 ft., including Nanda Devi (25,645 ft.), the highest peak in the Empire, and over a hundred lesser peaks all over 20,000 ft. To the east lies Nepal, on the west is the native state of Tehri Garhwal, and north is Tibet. The Tibetan border runs on the north side of the highest axis of elevation, the northern slopes of the range merging into the high Tibetan plateau, and south of the range are the foothills running down to the plains of British India. It is noteworthy that the watershed lies near the Tibetan border on the north side of the line of highest elevation, which would naturally be expected to form the watershed. The rivers have either cut back through the range or the country has been elevated since the existence of the rivers.

There are three main rivers flowing roughly south, cutting through the range at right angles, and between these river valleys are the chains containing the highest summits, forming, as it were, spurs thrown out from the main range. From east to west the rivers are the Gori, the Dhauli, and the Alaknanda. The last two flow into the Ganges, the

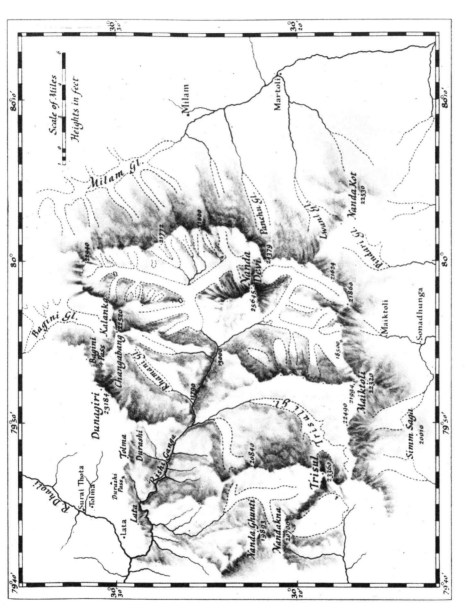

Map 2: Nanda Devi and her surroundings
By courtesy of the Royal Geographical Society

Alaknanda constituting one of its main sources, and at the head of all three valleys are high passes leading into Tibet. Between the Gori and the Dhauli lies the range containing Nanda Devi, and at its southern extremity this range bends round to the west towards Trisul (23,360 ft.), and culminates in Nandakna (20,700 ft.), and Nanda Ghunti (19,893 ft.). Some ten miles north of this abrupt westerly bend another spur of approximately equal length branches off, its western extremity marked by Dunagiri (23,184 ft.). Between these two short parallel spurs is a yet shorter one composing Nanda Devi itself, so that we have here a sort of reversed letter 'EC', the short middle stroke representing Nanda Devi, the longer top stroke the Dunagiri, and the bottom stroke the Trisul massif. But that is not all; subsidiary spurs branch off from Trisul and Dunagiri and converge upon the middle stroke, thus almost encircling Nanda Devi with a ring of mountains.

The space between the foot of Nanda Devi and its ring-fence of giant peaks, in extent some two hundred and fifty square miles, contains many lesser peaks and ridges, an extensive glacier system, rock, scree, and, surprisingly enough, grass slopes of wide extent. The whole is known as the Nanda Devi Basin, or more felicitously, the Sanctuary, a name first bestowed on it by Mr Ruttledge of Everest fame, who in the following passage graphically describes the unique situation of the mountain: 'Nanda Devi imposes on her votaries an admission test as yet beyond their skill and endurance. Surrounded by a barrier ring, 70 m. long, on which stand twelve measured peaks over 21,000 ft., and which nowhere descends lower than 18,000 ft., except in the West, where the Rishi Ganga river, rising at the foot of Nanda Devi, and the sole drainage for 250 sq. m. of ice and snow, has carved for itself what must be one of the most terrific gorges in the world. Two ridges converging on the river form as it were the curtain to an inner sanctuary within which the great mountain soars up to 25,645 ft. So tremendous is the aspect of the gorge that Hindu mythology described it as the last earthly home of the Seven Rishis—here if anywhere their meditations would be undisturbed.' The Rishis mentioned here were seven wise men, Hindu sages, and they are now said to be represented by the seven stars in the constellation of the Great Bear.

The superstitions, myths, and traditions, relating to mountains, are most of them interesting and some beautiful. The mountains of

Garhwal are particularly rich in such stories, because Garhwal is the birthplace of the Hindu religion, the traditional home of most of the gods of the Hindu Pantheon, and the terrestrial scene of their exploits. Every mountain and river, almost every rock and pool, is associated in legend with the life of some god.

Of the population of Garhwal, the orthodox among the immigrant Brahmans and Rajputs worship the five great gods, Vishnu, Siva, Devi, the Sun, and Ganesh, the elephant-headed god of wisdom. The bulk of the people, Khasiyas, a race of a caste lower than the Brahmans or the Rajputs, but yet generally allowed to be also immigrants from an Aryan source, adore principally the mountain god Siva; while the Doms, less than a fifth in number of the rest and believed to be the aborigines of the country, propitiate the local gods and demons who were in existence long before the coming of the Brahmans and Hinduism. But all, even the hillman such as the Bhotia, who has little respect for things sacred, find a common subject for reverence in the majesty and aloofness of the snowy ranges. At any sudden revelation of one of these giants, the home of one of the deities, coolie and priest alike will fold their hands and with bowed head utter a word of prayer.

Nor is worship at the high places of Himachal, 'the abode of snow' sacred to the Hindu gods, confined only to the nearer inhabitants. From all parts of India pilgrims make their way annually to this Hindu 'Palestine' to 'acquire merit' by enduring the privations of the road, and, by worshipping at the shrines, to receive forgiveness for past sins and assurance of future happiness.

At Kedarnath Siva, or Mahadeo, the god of everything destructive and terrible, is the object of adoration; at Badrinath the temple is dedicated to the benignant Vishnu, and a third famous shrine is found at Gangotri. All three lie amongst the great group of mountains which separate the valleys of the Bhagirathi and Alaknanda, rivers which unite a little lower down to form the Ganges.

At Kedarnath the tradition is that the god in the form of a buffalo took refuge from his pursuers the Pandavas (a tribe of the Dasyus who represent the original black race as opposed to the fair Aryans). For further safety he dived into the ground but left his hinder parts exposed, and a mountain there, in shape something like the less dangerous end of a buffalo, is still an object of adoration. The remaining parts of the god are worshipped at four other places along the Hima-layan chain; the arms at Tungnath, the face at Rudrnath, the belly at Madmahes-war, and the head at Kalpeswar. Together these five places form the 'Panch-Kedar', and to visit them in succession is a great ambition of the Hindu devotee, but one, I imagine, which is not often accomplished. I have in mind particularly Madmaheswar, which lies up a valley that few plainsmen would care to penetrate.

Bigoted followers of Siva or Vishnu visit only the temple dedi-cated to their respective god, but the great number of pilgrims make the round of as many of the sacred places as possible. Badrinath prob-ably receives the most, and derives from its fifty thousand annual visi-tors a far greater revenue than that of Kedarnath. Badrinath also has its five sacred places, the 'Panch-Badri', comprised within the Holy Circle of Badrinath, which extends from the shrine of Kanwa to the summit of Nanda Devi, on which there is a lake, the abode of Vishnu himself. The Bhagirathi, which is a lesser stream than the Alaknanda, has a greater reputation for sanctity, but it does not attract as many pil-grims as do the sources of the Alaknanda, particularly the fall of Bhas-udara. The temple of Gangotri is ten miles below the place where the Bhagirathi issues from the snout of the Gangotri glacier, a very holy spot called Gaumukh or the 'Cow's Mouth'. It is here that, according to Hindu mythology, the heaven-born goddess first descended upon earth. Water from the river at Gangotri, sealed in flasks by the Brah-man priests, is taken to the plains as being of great value.

Of the exact meaning of Nanda Devi, or rather of 'Nanda', it is not easy to get any precise information. According to one interpretation it means the 'Blessed' or 'Revered' Goddess, but if there is anything in a story I was told it means the goddess Nanda. Nanda was the daughter of a Kumaon king (Kumaon is a division of which Garhwal is part, and was formerly a separate native state) whose hand was demanded in marriage by a Rohilla prince. He was refused, and war followed, a battle taking place near Ranikhet. Nanda's kingly father was defeated and the future goddess fled and, after many vicissitudes, took refuge on the top of Nanda Devi. There are two other mountains in the vicin-ity in which the name 'Nanda' occurs. Nanda Ghunti to the west has already been mentioned and this, I was told, means 'The halting-place of Nanda'; it is only 19,893 ft. high and was probably used as a stepping

Trisul from summit of Nanda Devi

stone to Nanda Devi itself. To the east is Nanda Kot (22,500 ft.), which means 'The stronghold of Nanda', and south is Trisul, 'The Trident', a defiance to any rapacious Rohillas.

Amongst the local natives this belief that the mountains are the abode of gods and demons is less strong than it used to be. In 1830 Mr Traill, the first Commissioner, accompanied by local coolies, crossed a pass between Nanda Kot and Nanda Devi. The story goes that he suffered severely from snow-blindness, which the coolies attributed to the wrath of the goddess, and they affirmed that he only recovered after making an offering at the temple of Nanda Devi at Almora. The story may not be strictly accurate, but only a pedant would have it otherwise.

In 1855 the same route was taken by Adolph Schlagintweit, and of this crossing Mr A. L. Mumm in *Five Months in the Himalaya* related the following. A promise of additional pay and a rich offering to Nanda Devi had to be promised before any coolies could be persuaded to start. On top of the Pass, 'Schlagintweit commenced taking observations but was disagreeably interrupted by three of the hardiest men being seized with epileptic fits... A cry rose up that Nanda Devi had entered into them and Adolph, fearful lest the seizure might spread further, took aside two Brahmans whom he had with him, and after pointing out that he had given Nanda Devi all that they had demanded, and that this unpleasant scene was only the result of their own folly in calling on the goddess at every difficult place on the way up, ordered them to put a stop to it at once. This they achieved, partly by prayers, and partly by putting snow on the head of the sufferers, the latter remedy being, in Adolph's opinion, the more effective of the two.'

A later traveller, W. W. Graham, in 1883 had trouble with the local natives when he attempted to approach Nanda Devi by the gorge of the Rishis. His men all deserted, ostensibly on the grounds that the gorge was infested with devils. But in 1934 when Mr Shipton and the writer penetrated the gorge our Dotial and Bhotia coolies evinced no superstitious fears, though they, of course, are not really local men. Some men from the Dhauli valley whom we employed did desert, but I think the devils they feared were more tangible—the devils of discomfort and hard work. In 1936 we took a few coolies from a village at the very mouth of the Rishi Ganga and for them superstition either did not exist or was overcome, and this was the more remarkable because they came up the Rishi and joined us at the foot of the mountain, unaccompanied by any European.

On the other hand, shortly after our return, a local correspondent of a well-known Indian newspaper published a report to the following effect. In 1936 the monsoon rainfall was exceptionally heavy in the United Provinces and Garhwal, and on August 29th, after a severe storm, the Pindar river, which is fed by the glaciers of Nanda Kot and Trisul, rose many feet and wrought considerable havoc in the village of Tharali; a village, by the way, through which we had passed on the way to the mountain some weeks before. Forty lives were lost, several houses destroyed, and many cattle drowned. It was on the same day, August 29th, that we climbed the mountain and thus provoked the anger of the goddess, who immediately avenged, blindly but terribly, the violation of her sanctuary.

CHAPTER II

HISTORICAL

———————◆———————

THE READER WHO BLENCHES at the chapter heading will be pleased to hear that it is not necessary to recall the history of previous attempts on the mountain because there have not been any. For fifty years the problem which engaged the attention of many experienced mountaineers was not how to climb the mountain but how to reach it. But as the approach to the mountain was not the least serious of the problems which we had to face, perhaps it will not be out of place to outline briefly the story of these attempts, although they have already been recounted very thoroughly in Mr Shipton's *Nanda Devi*.

The truism that we climb on the shoulders of our predecessors is sometimes forgotten, and it is difficult to exaggerate the importance of the part which earlier failures play in the final success. The Himalayan peaks over, say, 23,000 ft. which have been climbed at the first attempt can be numbered on the fingers of one hand, and even if the present climb be cited to the contrary, the answer is that we had the inestimable advantage of knowing where to make our effort and how to get there—knowledge gained for us by our forerunners. And apart from previous experience on the actual mountain there is the vast fund of accumulated knowledge of high climbing in general to draw upon; for though experiences may be 'the name men give to their mistakes' it does not lessen their value to those who are willing to learn.

The earliest expedition was that of W. W. Graham in 1883, who was accompanied by two Swiss guides and who hoped to reach the mountain by way of the Rishi gorge. This river, as has already been said, drains the whole of the Nanda Devi Basin. It has two sources at the snouts of the two glaciers encircling the north-east and south-west sides of the mountain, and the streams from these glaciers unite at the foot of the west ridge. From this point the river, by now a formidable torrent, flows west through a gorge or series of gorges until after a distance of about eight miles it joins the Dhauli river near the village of

28

Rini. Graham's party started to follow the river up from near its junction with the Dhauli, but were stopped almost at once by the difficulty of the terrain; nor to this day has anyone succeeded in passing the lower portals of the gorge.

Repulsed here Graham and his two guides, Boss and Kaufmann, moved round to the north and, after an unsuccessful attempt on Dunagiri, learnt from shepherds that there was a way into the Rishi *nala* over the northern containing wall which avoided the insuperable difficulties of the lower four miles. 'On the evening of the second day', Graham wrote, 'we reached a lovely little table-land called Dunassau (Durashi). The last day's route had been extremely wild running along the southern face of the ridge, sometimes with a sheer drop to the river below—some 7000 to 8000 feet. Such wild rocks and broken gullies I had never met before.' Here most of their coolies deserted, but they pushed on: 'Occasionally we had to hang on to a tuft of grass or a bunch of Alpine roses, and I do not exaggerate when I say that for half the day's work hand-hold was as necessary as foot-hold.' Several days of this sort of work brought them to a place where they were finally stopped by the smooth cliffs of the north side and inability to cross the river to the more accommodating south bank. The desertion of their remaining coolies put an end to their hopes and they abandoned their loads and struggled back as best they could.

In 1905 Dr Longstaff, a name for ever associated with mountain exploration in Garhwal, attacked the problem from the opposite side. In that year he and two Italian guides, the Brocherel brothers, were in the Gori valley to the east of the Nanda Devi massif with designs on East Nanda Devi (24,300 ft.). This mountain is the highest of the encircling peaks and from it extends that short ridge, the middle stroke of the reversed letter 'E', which links it with Nanda Devi itself. Starting from Milam in the Gori valley Longstaff's party got on to the rim of the Basin at the foot of the south-east shoulder of the lesser Nanda Devi, at a height of 19,100 ft. They were thus the first ever to look down into the mysterious sanctuary; but the descent looked formidable, nor was it their objective. It had been a close thing, but the Sanctuary remained inviolate.

In 1907 Dr Longstaff returned to the attack with a strong party which included General Bruce, Mr Mumm, and three Alpine guides.

Their first attempt was by what Dr Longstaff called the 'back door', the route which Graham had learnt of from the shepherds. Half-way up the gorge from Rini on the north side of the river, and a couple of thousand feet above it, there are two hanging valleys. Here is valuable grazing to which, in the summer, are brought the sheep and goats from many neighbouring villages, some enterprising but unknown shepherd of a bygone age having found a remarkable route to these alps, or Kharaks, as they are called locally. The route involves the crossing of a 14,000 ft. pass which in late spring is still snow-covered, and a rather hair-raising, or since sheep form the bulk of the travellers, wool-raising, traverse across a mile of cliffs. The pass, however, was found to be still blocked by snow, so the party moved round to the north and east of Dunagiri and proceeded up the Bagini glacier in an attempt to cross the northern wall of the Basin, the top stroke of our reversed 'Ǝ'. There was a pass at the head of this glacier which according to the map then in use should have led into the Basin, but this region of ice and snow had of course not been included in the survey, and though the map did credit to the maker's imagination it was apt to mislead. The map of Garhwal in use up to 1936 was made from a survey in 1868 which was, rightly, only carried up to the snow-line, and above this, not so rightly, it was largely filled in by guess-work. There is nothing but praise and thankfulness for the accuracy of the surveyed portion, but for the unsurveyed part we should all prefer to have a map which, like the crew of the Snark, we can all understand, 'a perfect and absolute blank'. In 1934 we had the same experience as Dr Longstaff's party in other parts of Garhwal. From an explorer's point of view it may seem inconsistent and ungracious to gird at inadequate maps, for it is the explorer's job to fill them in. But this is only a plea for blanks instead of fancy; blanks, of which there are, alas, but few remaining, thanks to the energy of the Indian Survey. At the present moment a new survey of Garhwal is in hand, and this year (1936) we had the advantage of a provisional new issue of the old map incorporating the results of much private and official work done in Garhwal in recent years. Is it not time to start a Society for the Suppression and Abolition of Maps and Guide Books, not necessarily confined to the Himalaya? With the accumulation of exact knowledge comes the desire to put it to use, and we shall presently have a Five-Year Plan for the Himalaya and learn that the Sanctuary is one of those eligible sites 'ripe for development'. To show that this is not completely idle fancy I might mention that 'Pilgrimage by Air' is, if not an actual fact, at least an advertised one. The following appeared in *The Times* dated from Delhi this year: 'An aerodrome among the Himalayas, 10,500 ft. above sea-level, is being constructed by the Air Transport Company here to cope with the pilgrim traffic to the Badrinath shrine, sacred to the Hindus. The present terminus (long may it remain so) of the air route to the shrine is situated at Gauchar, about 70 miles from Hard-war. The return journey between Hardwar (sic) and Gauchar takes about eight weeks by road, and could be done in twelve hours by rail.' The words in parenthesis are the author's. For Hardwar, in the last sentence, I suggest read Badrinath; we have been told the distance is seventy miles, and four weeks for the single journey is a little slow even for a pilgrim travelling on his hands and knees or measuring his length on the ground at every step, as some of them do.

To return to our exploring party on top of the Bagini pass; they found, after crossing the pass and descending another glacier, that they had got into the Rishi gorge at the point reached by Graham and were still separated by three miles of cliff from the inner Sanctuary. Shortage of food compelled them to hurry with all speed down the Rishi instead of attempting to force this upper passage, and they finally emerged by the 'back door', which was now clear of snow. After a rest they came up the Rishi once more and Dr Longstaff with two of the guides (the Brocherel brothers) climbed Trisul, going from a camp at 17,500 ft. to the top in one day—an amazing tour de force which is not likely to be repeated.

Trisul was climbed on June 12th, and the 14th saw Dr Longstaff and two Gurkhas trying to force a way up the south bank of the Rishi. Foiled here, they crossed to the north side by a natural rock bridge and camped near the entrance of the Rhamani torrent down which they had come on the previous journey recounted above. The height was 11,700 ft., and the next day they climbed to 13,500 ft. up the cliffs of the north bank, but found this side even less encouraging than the other. In view of the difficulties and at the instance of other plans still to be carried out, no further attempt was made to penetrate the grim defile and Dr Longstaff rejoined his party in the lower Rishi.

In 1932 Mr Ruttledge, who as Deputy Commissioner of the Almora
district had had opportunities for studying the problem of Nanda Devi
and the Basin both from distant Almora and from journeys to the east
and north, thought that he had discovered a breach in the outer ram-
part. About half-way round the southern rim from Trisul to East Nanda
Devi the surrounding wall falls to its lowest elevation, about 18,000 ft.
or slightly less. From a distance this depression seemed a likely place
for a crossing of the wall, but rising as it did from a deep and steep
valley very little of the approach to it could be seen. Accompanied
by Émile Rey, an Italian guide, and six Sherpa porters, Mr Ruttledge
went up the Maiktoli valley to get a closer look, but from beneath so
forbidding was the aspect of the proposed pass that not even a closer
inspection was required.

'We were brought up all-standing by a sight which almost took
our remaining breath away. Six thousand feet of the steepest rock
and ice... Near the top of the wall, for about a mile and a half, runs
a terrace of ice some 200 feet thick. Under the pull of gravity large
masses constantly break off from this terrace and thunder down to the
valley below, polishing in their fall the successive bands of limestone
of which the face is composed. Even supposing the precipice to be
climbable, an intelligent mountaineer may be acquitted on a charge
of lack of enterprise if he declines to spend at least three days and two
nights under fire from this artillery. As alternative, there is a choice of
three knife-edge arêtes, excessively steep, sometimes overhanging in
the middle and lower sections, on which even the eye of faith, assisted
by binoculars, fails to see one single platform large enough to accom-
modate the most modest of climbing tents.

'The jury's verdict was unanimous; and so vanished the last hope
of a straightforward approach to Nanda Devi; and the goddess keeps
her secret.'

Prior to this Mr Ruttledge had made two previous attempts. One
in 1926 accompanied by Dr Howard Somervell and Major-General
R. C. Wilson, when an approach by the Timphu glacier to the north-
east was tried but found to be even more hopeless than that by the
south or west. And again in 1927 with Dr Longstaff, when the lowest
point of the wall, 17,000 ft., at the head of the Nandakini valley to the
south-west was reached. Further progress was barred by bad weather,

Maiktoli Pass (crossed 1934) and Maiktoli Peak, 22,350 ft.

but this approach would but have led into the lower Rishi Ganga and not into the Basin.

In 1934 Mr Shipton and the writer with three Sherpa porters went to Garhwal, having as our main objective the entrance and mapping of the Basin. As with a man making a second marriage, hope triumphed over experience, and by Dr Longstaff's advice we directed our attention to the Rishi gorge. The gorge was passed and a month was spent exploring and mapping the Promised Land of the Basin, and in the autumn a second journey was made to complete the work. On this second occasion a way out was found over the low depression in the southern wall but, of course, in the reverse direction to that which Mr Ruttledge had intended, and in consequence a much simpler affair.

In the course of the six weeks spent in the Basin we had ample opportunity to study the mountain from every side. As a result of this study, having exhausted all other possibilities, we concluded rather unhopefully that a lodgement could be effected on the south ridge, but it seemed unlikely that the ridge would 'go'.*

We took a camp up the south-east glacier to within striking distance and, fully expecting that a closer acquaintance would only strengthen our first impressions, we devoted a day to the ridge. We reached a height of about 20,000 ft. and found it easier than we expected, which only goes to show the value of an oft-quoted piece of mountaineering advice by Dr Longstaff, that 'you must go and rub your nose in a place before being certain that it won't "go"'. It was a perfect autumn day and we sat for some time on our airy perch, following in imagination a route up the ever-steepening southern ridge, and fascinated by the grand sweep of the horse-shoe cirque at the head of the glacier, a 3000 ft. glacis of glittering ice. Despite our height and the clear day we were not well placed for judging the difficulties of the ridge above our heads. We were looking at it *en face*, we were too close, and the whole was very much foreshortened, but with due allowance for this our opinion was summed up by Mr Shipton in *Nanda Devi* as follows: 'The ridge was certainly showing signs of becoming more difficult but for the next few hundred feet there did not appear to be any

---

* 'Go'—a useful climbing idiom meaning not that the ridge went anywhere but that a climber could go up the ridge.

insuperable obstacles, and we came to the definite conclusion that if a well-equipped party were to spend a couple of weeks over the job there was a good chance that the ridge could be followed to the summit. It would be no easy task and the party would have to be supremely fit and competent.'

Two things may be noted in this brief summary: first, that Sherpa porters made their first appearance in Garhwal in 1927 with Mr Rut-tledge, for it was not until after the earlier Everest expeditions that the possibilities of these men were realised. The first travellers in Garhwal, like Traill and Graham, had only the local natives as porters, and these could only be relied upon below the snow-line, and not always then. Later their place was taken by European guides, an infinitely stronger substitute but a monstrously expensive one. Secondly, that the par-ties become successively smaller, ending with two Europeans and three Sherpas, for with a problem such as the approach to Nanda Devi the advantage lies obviously with the smaller party. I might add that in the last case smallness was dictated almost as much by motives of economy as of mobility.

When attempting a high mountain the party may have to be larger, but how much larger, if any, is a debatable point, and we still have what for convenience may be called 'Big-endians' and 'Little-endians' with us in the mountaineering world. A great deal must depend on the peak to be tackled, but there is no question which is the best for purposes of mountain exploration as opposed to an attack on a single peak. It may be thought that the expedition to be described, compris-ing eight Europeans, was a successful reversion to type, but apart from the number of climbers (actually seven) there was nothing big about it and in the course of the narrative it will appear that there is every justi-fication for classifying it as small.

CHAPTER III

PRELIMINARIES

W HEN AN EXPEDITION is on foot a certain amount of preliminary
work, proportionate to the size, has to be done. For some the
whole of the winter may be all too short for this, while, on the other
hand, I think the preparations for our two-man show in 1934 could, if
necessary, have been completed in one day. However, for those concerned with the organisation of something which intends calling itself
an 'expedition', the winter is a busy time, and since it is the custom to
be very reticent about plans, the organisers meet and go about their
business with the air of conspirators. One reason for this is that it is
annoying, or ought to be, to read in the Press of what an expedition is
going to do before it has even started; nor is it any consolation to know
that the information bears as much relation to fact as an official com-
muniqué did during the War.

The notion of a British-American expedition to the Himalaya was
first mooted in America, and plans were very far advanced before any
climbers on this side were approached. The objective was Kangchenjunga, the third highest peak in the world, and preparations were
on a correspondingly large scale. It was not until February 1936 that
W. F. Loomis came to England to collect four climbers, more equipment, and, most important of all, to apply to the Indian Government
for permission to go.

This was cutting it rather fine, for no one, least of all a Government, likes to be bounced into making quick decisions, and if they are
so bounced the decision is usually unfavourable. Fortunately we were
warned that such might be the case and we selected Nanda Devi as a
second string for our bow. Here, as has been explained, there were no
political complications, and moreover, for this objective, we had the
goodwill of all who had had anything to do with the mountain.

Meanwhile, Loomis having drawn up two equipment lists, one of
rather staggering dimensions for Kangchenjunga and a more modest

one for Nanda Devi, returned to the States, leaving me to collect our Nanda Devi requirements and to await the result of our application before ordering the rest.

The British party was now complete and comprised, in addition to the writer, T. Graham Brown, F.R.S., an eminent physiologist, who has climbed in the Alps for many years and who was one of the party which in 1934 climbed Mt Foraker (17,300 ft.), a difficult peak in Alaska, for the first time; N. E. Odell, a geologist, who in 1924 climbed twice to Camp VI (27,000 ft.) on Everest, and who, in addition to the Alps, has climbed in Spitsbergen, Labrador, and the Rockies. And lastly Peter Lloyd, another experienced Alpine climber with many fine guideless ascents to his credit, and a brilliant rock climber.

How many of the original American members would go was still uncertain and much depended on what our objective was to be. It was decided that the party should assemble in India at the end of June, as this was the earliest by which most of them could arrive. This was of course unusually late, for at that time the monsoon would already be active, but according to the experience of two German expeditions this would be no disadvantage for Kangchenjunga. July and August were said to be the most favourable months, the reason given being that prior to the monsoon particularly severe winds were the rule. For Nanda Devi the advantages of climbing during the monsoon were not very obvious, indeed anyone who had seen the mountain and knew the conditions in the gorge would consider that our chance of success was in consequence materially diminished.

It was important that one of us should go out to India in advance to collect porters and arrange transport, so I decided to leave in March, hoping that before then we should know whether we were going to Sikkim or Garhwal, seven or eight hundred miles apart. But it was not to be, and when I sailed at the end of the month, accompanied by only part of the food and equipment, the oracle at the India Office had not yet spoken. For my part I sailed in the hope and expectation that we would be permitted to try Kangchenjunga, mainly because for me it would be new ground. But correspondence with the others gave me the impression that they were prepared for a refusal with a most Christian-like resignation; in fact, I suspected they might even welcome it. To them both mountains were new, but there was more freshness and

originality about Garhwal and Nanda Devi. Kangchenjunga is seen by
everyone who goes to Darjeeling, various parties have prowled around
it, and it has received three full-dress assaults, and possibly to their
minds it was getting a bit moth-eaten. And moreover, though both
mountains gave us an equal chance of putting up a good show, there
was vast inequality in the chance of getting to the top; Kangchenjunga
is probably as formidable as Everest.

We tied up at Calcutta on a Monday, and a blacker, in both senses,
I have seldom experienced. The first letter to be opened informed me,
with regret, that the British-American Himalayan Expedition would
not be permitted to enter Sikkim to attempt Kangchenjunga; like most
oracular pronouncements no reasons were given. It seemed a pity to
have to accept this fiat without some protest, but there was nothing to
be done except write a 'forlorn hope' of a letter asking for reconsidera-
tion and the reply to that was merely an official 'raspberry'.

I now went round to see the Customs, for the Indian Government very generously allow expeditionary equipment to come in free
of duty. We had already written asking to be accorded this privilege,
but unfortunately no instructions had yet been received from Simla, so
nothing could be disembarked. Feeling a bit subdued, I thought it was
time to enlist some local aid and began hunting up the few people I
knew in Calcutta. All were either in England or Darjeeling and, feeling
more like a pariah every minute, I slunk away to a hotel. On the way
I noticed one or two people staring rather hard and, looking down,
I discovered a dark blue sea of ink the size of a plate on an otherwise
spotless white coat. At the hotel I handed it over to a boy telling him
to get busy with milk, lemon juice, india-rubber, and any other ink-
remover he knew. An hour later it was brought back, but not by the
same boy, and one soon understood why, for the last state was worse
than the first, the inky sea being now suffused over half the coat, and
though the deep rich blue had paled to a watery grey the effect was still
too bizarre for me to carry off.

My suit-case had now arrived, and in it another exciting discov-
ery awaited me in the shape of the havoc wrought by an uncorked
bottle of ink. Few things had escaped unmarked, and for the next few
days I must have looked a bit mottled because in a temperature of 100
degrees colour is apt to run. But soon a wire from Simla allowed me to

South face of Nanda Devi from across South-East glacier (Aug. 1936)

land and store the equipment and to escape from the Turkish bath of Calcutta in April to the freshness of Darjeeling.

The question was what to do, for now there was no preparatory work to be done in Sikkim, and the others would not arrive in India for nearly two months. There was the possibility of making a journey into the Basin to form a dump, but I had only a small amount of the food with me and, further, there was always the chance that bad weather might prevent the main body getting through and necessitate a change of plans—we should look uncommonly foolish if all our food was inside the Basin and we outside unable to reach it. Nor was it weather alone that might bring about this contingency; the first burst of the monsoon might break the slender thread of the route through the gorge by rock-falls or by washing off from the underlying slabs the thin covering of earth and grass upon which one depends mainly for holds. The most useful way of spending the time seemed to be to go into Sikkim with a few Sherpa porters to test their abilities, and then to take them up with me to Garhwal at the end of June.

For a stay of more than a fortnight in Sikkim a pass has to be obtained from Gangtok, the capital, and, being in a hurry, I was unwise enough to wire for this without explaining my intentions. The name must have aroused suspicion, for the reply was a request for full particulars of my intended journey; evidently I was regarded, figuratively, as the thin end of a British-American wedge. Telegrams were abandoned in favour of the type-writer and various other people were written to for assistance in this crisis. As a friend remarked, if the pen is mightier than the sword, the type-writer is mightier than the ice-axe. All Himalayan expeditions should carry one, even if it means leaving their ice-axes behind.

After a week's delay I started with four Sherpas, obtained only with difficulty. Even in England it had been clear that good porters would be hard to come by, and this was found to be true enough. The Everest expedition had of course skimmed the cream, a French expedition had taken thirty Sherpas to the Karakoram, and there was a small British party in Sikkim with another twenty. In consequence it was difficult to scrape together even four, and two of these were complete novices. On the eve of a long-delayed start a cable was received saying that Loomis would arrive in Bombay on May 21st, and asking if a journey into the Basin could be done before the monsoon began. A reply was sent advising him to wait and come out with the others, and then we made a double march from Darjeeling which put me well beyond the reach of any more cables.

After an all too brief but peaceful fortnight on the glaciers south of Kangchenjunga, I began worrying about what was happening and decided to return to Darjeeling, where we arrived on the 21st. Sure enough there was a letter to say that they had not been able to get in touch with Loomis to stop him and that he would be in Bombay on the 21st. Something had to be done, and now, contrary to previous notions, I thought it might as well be done in Garhwal. If we went straight there and moved fast we might be able to take some loads into the Basin and get back in time to organise the main party as well. By doing this we should have fewer loads to take in after the monsoon had started, and the party would therefore be less cumbersome; during this Sikkim trip the weather had been such as to remind me forcibly how unpleasant conditions might be in the monsoon, so that the fewer coolies we then had with us the better. I forget how many wires I sent to Bombay, for I did not know where Loomis was and feared he might have already started for Sikkim. The American Consul, all the Travel Agencies, and the Shipping Line, seemed a wide enough net, and next day I had the satisfaction of knowing that I had caught him.

We arranged by wire to meet in Ranikhet on May 28th.

Some arrangement had now to be made about the Sherpas. Of the four, I had already decided that only one was worth a place on a serious show; this was Pasang Kikuli, who was quite outstanding. He had been to Everest in 1933 and carried to Camp V, where he got slightly frost-bitten hands, but having been treated with oxygen suffered no ill-effects. He had also been twice to Kangchenjunga and was on Nanga Parbat in 1934, where he was one of the five porters to get down alive from the highest camp, six porters and three Europeans dying on the mountain. It was strange that he should have been overlooked by the Everest and other parties, but their loss was our gain, and he turned out to be a treasure. When the time came for me to leave Darjeeling no more porters had come in, so I took two of the original four, one of course Pasang Kikuli, and left instructions for four more to be sent up later when there might be some more likely candidates available.

Pasang's companion was one Pasang Phuta, a good average porter but with no outstanding qualities except a disarming grin. The Americans called him a bit 'dumb', and anyone who knew Pasang Phuta would not need to be told that this is a briefer way of saying that he was not highly endowed mentally.

CHAPTER IV

A TELEGRAM TO THE TEMPLE

R ANIKHET, WHITHER WE WERE NOW BOUND, is a hill station in the
United Provinces. From Kathgodam, thirty-six hours' journey by
train from Calcutta, it is reached by a good road of fifty miles. Numerous
buses ply on this fifty-mile stretch of road and competition is so fierce
that the fare is only three shillings, luggage included, and perhaps an
extra sixpence for the doubtful privilege of sitting next to the driver.

Ranikhet is 6000 ft. above sea level, and the relief on reaching it
and breathing the pine-scented air, after a journey by rail through the
sweltering plains, has to be felt to be believed. On many days of the
year this feeling of having left hell and arrived somewhere near heaven
is intensified by the sight of a hundred and more miles of snow peaks:
distant, it is true, but near enough to stagger by their height and fasci-
nate by their purity. At this time of year though, before the monsoon,
they are seldom seen to advantage, owing to the dust haze which drifts
up from the plains.

Apart from the view there are no distractions for the casual visitor
to Ranikhet, and this was as well, because we had no time to waste.
We had to get up the Rishi gorge, into the Basin if possible, and I had
decided that we must be back by June 25th, in order that we could
have things well in hand before the others arrived.

Normally it would take eighteen days to get there, not allowing
for any delay *en route*, and in this case delay was almost inevitable. The
food and equipment which I had brought out was still on the way up
from Calcutta by goods train and none of the American consignments
had yet arrived, so that the only loads we could take were coolie food,
which could be bought locally; that is rice, atta (wheat flour), and satu,
for feeding the local coolies on the way in and the Sherpas while on
the mountain. Satu is the same thing as the Tibetan tsampa—barley,
or wheat, which has been parched and then ground into meal. It has
one great advantage in that it needs little or no cooking; you can put

43

it in tea and make it into a thick paste, or moisten it very slightly with water and mould it into a cake; it can even be eaten dry, but that is not a method I can honestly recommend. It also makes an excellent porridge, and, if there is a little milk to help it down, tastes more like food than some of the shavings and sawdust sold as cereals. This food could be bought at Joshimath, nine marches from Ranikhet, so there was no need to take any coolies until Joshimath was reached. These men I proposed getting from Mana, a little village in the extreme north-west of Garhwal near the Tibet border. It was only twenty-one miles from Joshimath, and men from there had been up the Rishi with Shipton and me in 1934, and their stoutness and rock-climbing ability were beyond all question.

If delay was to be avoided these arrangements had to be made before we left Ranikhet, because it would take time to collect 900 lb. of food and to get the men down from Mana to Joshimath. Fortunately this could be done.

There is a telegraph line to Joshimath, and a wire and a money order to a man in the bazaar there set on foot the collecting of the food. There remained the problem of the porters. Mana is twenty-one miles from Joshimath, and to go up there, find the men, and return, would take a good three days. But the problem was solved in a rather unlikely way by invoking the aid of the priesthood.

The telegraph line does not stop at Joshimath but follows the Pilgrim Road up to Badrinath, which is only three miles short of Mana. Of Badrinath, the Mecca for fifty thousand Hindu pilgrims, something has already been said. It consists of a temple, a number of pilgrim rest-houses, and shops, situated in an open valley on the right bank of the Alaknanda river, only twenty-five miles below the Mana Pass into Tibet. The fall of Bhasadura, one of the sacred sources, where 'the Ganges falls like the thread of a Lotus flower', is not far away, and there are bathing pools in the river, and thermal springs, which are all efficacious in cleansing believers of past offences.

The temple, however, is the centre around which the life of Badrinath revolves during the short pilgrim season between May and October. Badrinath is 10,280 ft. above the sea, and during the winter snow lies everywhere, the temple is closed, and the officials, shopkeepers and others migrate to a less inhospitable clime. The temple is close to the river. It has a very modern appearance, but the foundation dates from the eighth century and the first building is said to have been erected by Sankara Acharya, the great Hindu reformer. This building and several subsequent ones are believed to have been destroyed by avalanches but, considering its situation, this is difficult to understand unless great changes have taken place in the formation of the surrounding country. The idol in the main temple is of black stone, stands about three feet high and is clothed with rich brocade, and wears a tiara of gold in which is a large diamond. The dresses and ornaments are reputed to be worth at least ten thousand rupees. The idol is served daily with two meals, and after a decent interval has elapsed the food is distributed amongst the pilgrims, many of whom are too poor to feed themselves. Offerings are of course made by the pilgrims in cash, kind, or ornaments, according to their means; strict accounts are kept by the treasurers, and the business affairs of the temple are in the hands of a secretary. Other members of the temporal council for the affairs of the Badrinath temple are the Bhotias of Mana, so that this village is intimately connected with its larger neighbour.

At the height of the pilgrim season the scene in the one narrow street of Badrinath brings back memories of Kim. Wealthy babus in 'jhampans', or dandies, carried by four sweating coolies, the more economically minded in long cylindrical baskets carried by only one; old men and women of all classes arriving on foot travel-stained and weary, clutching their pilgrim's staff; all welcomed by a roll of drums nicely proportioned in length and loudness to the probable state of the pilgrim's purse; naked fakirs smeared with ashes, long-haired saddhus, blind and deformed beggars thrusting their wooden bowls under the nose of every shopkeeper in the bazaar, getting here a little flour or a handful of rice, there some spices or salt, and nowhere a refusal; all these jostle each other in the narrow stone-flagged street between the open-fronted shops where yak-tails and Manchester cottons, musk and cheap photographs lie huddled together; and over all, aloof, watchful, stand the snows of Himachal where the gods live.

To find amongst all this a Post and Telegraph Office savours of banality if not impropriety, but to us it proved invaluable. In 1934 Shipton and I had twice visited Badrinath and made the acquaintance of the Rawal or Priest of the temple (to give him his full title, His

Holiness the Rawal Pandit Basudeva Numbudri), a high-caste Brahman from Southern India. This custom of appointing a Brahman from the south as the Rawal of a temple in the northernmost confines of India dates back to about A.D. 800, when the great Hindu reformer, Sankara Acharya, drove out encroaching Bhuddism from Garhwal and took measures, of which this was one, to maintain the purity of the restored religion. It was this same Sankara who preached the efficacy of the pilgrimage to the holy places of the Himalaya. I was now reminded of this friend in need and felt confident that a wire to him, asking for a dozen Mana men to be sent to Joshimath on June 6th, would be all that was needed.

One more day was spent in Ranikhet having a big tarpaulin made up, buying a few necessities, and arranging for a bus. In the course of the day a reply came from Joshimath assuring us that the food would be ready. None of our equipment had yet arrived, a fact which made it the more easy to travel as light as we intended.

My sleeping bag, which had an inner and outer lining, would do for both of us, the tarpaulin would cover the food, the two Sherpas, and ourselves, while extra clothing was not wanted as we would not be going above 14,000 ft.

So on May 30th, two days after arriving, we started out, the party consisting of two Sherpas, a 10 lb. Cheddar cheese, and ourselves. The cheese was one out of a case of six which I had luckily brought up from Calcutta in my own compartment to spare them the prolonged suffering of a ten-day journey by goods train in the hot weather.

From Ranikhet you can get a flying start in a bus, and this dropped us fifty miles away at a place called Garul, where the road ended, by half-past ten in the morning. The height of this place is only 3000 ft., and Gwaldam, where we stopped for the night, is over 3000 ft. higher and ten miles away. It was fairly cool, thanks to a dust cloud which hid the sun, but otherwise this march can be a trying one. At Gwaldam a bungalow welcomes the traveller. That and a few unhappy looking tea bushes are the only remaining evidence of a once flourishing tea estate. It rained hard in the night, but next day we were permitted to remain dry until two o'clock, when it began again with some violence. A fair interval persuaded us to push on from the village where we were sheltering to the next stream, and there we got our tarpaulin rigged

Entrance to the Temple, Badrinath

just before another deluge began. It was open at both ends, and when the four of us were lying cheek by jowl there was a foot or two to spare at each end—on fine nights the outer berth was very desirable. Rain in Garhwal may be heavy, but usually it seems to be unaccompanied by wind and the tarpaulin kept us dry very effectively.

When reading accounts of travel in Garhwal the peculiar nature of the country should be borne in mind. The whole country is an intricate tangle of valleys and ridges with their attendant ravines and spurs, which, even in the foothills, are all on a scale undreamt of in this country. The stages of a march may seem short, but involving, as most of them do, a rise of 3000 ft. or more and an equally great descent, they are quite long enough. It is possible to be in a valley not more than 3000 ft. above the sea, the home of a vegetation which is almost tropical, and at the same time to be within fifteen miles of snow-clad peaks 20,000 ft. high.

The following story seems to me to provide as apt an illustration of the country now as it did then. 'In the reign of Akbar, that prince demanded of the Raja of Srinagar (the ancient capital of Garhwal) an account of the revenues of his raj and a chart of his country. The Raja being then at court, repaired to the presence the following day and in obedience to the commands of the king presented a true statement of his finances and a chart of his country by introducing a lean camel and saying: "This is a faithful picture of the territory I possess—up and down and very poor." The king smiled at the ingenuity of the thought and told him that from the revenues of a country produced with so much labour and in amount so small, he had nothing to demand.' It was over the humps and hollows of the camel's back that we had now to pass. There are three possible routes from Ranikhet to Joshimath and we took the most easterly, which is the one generally used and one which has been frequently described. It is supposedly the shortest, but that is doubtful, for it certainly involves more climbing than the other two. There are three big valleys between Garul and Joshimath, all running from east to west directly across the route; the valley of the Pindar river which comes from the south of Nanda Kot, the Nandakini from the slopes of Trisul, and the Bireh Ganga from Nanda Ghunti; and naturally the farther east and the nearer the mountains these are crossed, the higher are the intervening ridges.

The most westerly route is the Pilgrim Road, which avoids crossing any of these valleys by following the main valley of the Alaknanda.
It is usually shunned by expeditions, at any rate on the outward journey, on account of the risk of picking up dysentery, cholera, or malaria;
curiously enough these diseases seem to lose their terrors when the
expedition is on the way home. It is provided with bungalows at every
stage and a variety of food can be bought, which perhaps explains the
curious fact noted above; whereas on the route we took there is only
one bungalow and no food. We had brought from Ranikhet for our
own use rice, lentils, and flour, sufficient to last until Joshimath, but
the Sherpas, expecting to be able to buy at every village, had brought
very little. For most of the way all they could get was barley flour, and
it became quite pathetic to hear them asking, hopefully but vainly, at
every house they passed for wheat flour.

Eggs and milk were our desideratum, but this was a much fonder
hope than that entertained by the Sherpas for their atta. The absence
of eggs is understandable because to Hindus hens are unclean and are
seldom kept, for in some ways the Garhwali is a very orthodox Hindu.
Sometimes one comes across ex-soldiers who have served the British
Raj in the Garhwal Rifles who have so far lost caste that they are sufficiently abandoned to keep hens. The rarity with which milk could be
got is less easily explained. Every village possessed livestock in abun-
dance, cows, water buffalo, goats; and one could not help thinking
that it was the will to help which was lacking, not the ability.

This wet night in a forest glade was a dismal one owing to a new
brand of midges, new at least to me. An ordinary midge observes regu-
lar hours and knocks off as soon as darkness sets in, but here they carried on business all night long without intermission—if you left your
head out you were driven frantic, and suffocated if you put it inside the
sleeping bag.

Next day we crossed a pass on the ridge between the Pindar and
Nandakini valleys at about 10,000 ft. and dropped down through oak
and rhododendron forest and grassy alps to Kanol. It was just too
late in the year to see the rhododendrons in flower, which are at their
best early in May; they are found between 8000 and 10,000 ft., and
this route is particularly rich in this gorgeous kind of forest—gorgeous
when in flower, but in other seasons drab and grey. It rained again all

the afternoon, and an inside that was far from well added to my gloom; but apart from that we had good reason to be pleased because we were already a day ahead of time. It required a desperate effort next day to retain this lead, for the usual bridge over the Nandakini had gone, and a long detour, five miles up stream and five down again, had to be made. Then we got into trouble crossing a smaller river, where the bridge consisted of the usual two pine logs and flat stones in between. Those with experience are careful to stick to the logs, but Loomis trusted to the stones, which naturally slipped through and in he went, losing both topee and ice-axe. Pasang Kikuli recaptured the topee after an exciting race down stream, and we wasted half an hour at the pool below the bridge while Loomis stripped, tied on the climbing rope, and methodically searched the bottom of the pool for the axe. The loss of this axe led to the loss of another, nor was the topee destined to live much longer.

We finally made the appointed stage late that evening, wet, weary, and cold, the result of a very violent hailstorm which we had encountered. In my infirm state I was glad to find shelter in a sort of rest-house; it had a mud floor and no furniture, but a roof and an excellent fireplace made up for these deficiencies.

The next obstacle was the Bireh Ganga, across which we were relieved to find there was still a bridge albeit with little to spare between it and the surging water. I began to wonder how we would fare six weeks later when the river would certainly be very much higher. Our camp that night was amongst some large erratic boulders near the village of Kaliaghat, and a convenient rock overhang preserved our fire from what was now the inevitable afternoon rain. It seemed that the monsoon had already broken, but we talked ourselves into believing that this was merely the 'chota Barsat', the little rains, which are supposed to precede the monsoon proper.

The last and highest ridge was yet to be crossed, that between the Bireh Ganga and the Alaknanda valley in which lies Joshimath itself. The way over this ridge is by the well-known Kuari Pass, 12,400 ft., which is usually crossed on the second day's march from Kaliaghat. We, however, put on steam and reached Dekwani, the camping place at the foot of the Pass, by midday, and went up and over in the afternoon.

Dekwani is a grazing ground just above the tree-line and 1000 ft. below the Pass, and that day there must have been at least a thousand

Below the Kuari Pass

sheep and goats present. It lies on a route which is much used by sheep and goat transport into Tibet. This route follows the Dhauli valley down from the Niti Pass (16,600 ft.) and, leaving the valley short of Joshimath, crosses the Kuari Pass and so reaches the southern valleys of Garhwal. It is a route favourable to such a form of transport because it is high and cool, there is plenty of grass, and few villages. Grain is the usual commodity carried going up to Tibet and salt and borax on the return. A sheep can carry about 20 lb. and a big goat 30 lb., so that a flock of one hundred, which is a small one, can shift a ton or more. The saddle bags are made of coarse wool or hemp strengthened with leather, and are carefully balanced on the back and secured by what corresponds to a breastplate and a crupper; there is no girth. When halted the saddle bags are stacked into a high wall which affords some shelter to the drovers.

We halted at Dekwani to have some food and pass the time of day with the sheep drovers. They were inclined to be surly and took time to thaw out; in fact when the Sherpas borrowed their fire to boil some water they spat ostentatiously and muttered imprecations. A little tobacco soon mollified them, for these Bhotias are inveterate smokers, smoking stuff which looks for all the world like plum pudding, and smoking charcoal rather than nothing at all.

From Dekwani we were on top of the Pass in fifty minutes, but of the glorious view which often rewards the early morning traveller there was no sign. Lowering clouds and mist veiled the horizon in all directions and when, an hour later, we camped below the tree-line these burst in furious squalls of wind and rain. In the evening when the rain stopped we were able to appreciate the best camping ground we had yet had. A smooth flat carpet of grass to lie on, a sparkling brook at our feet, unlimited firewood for the gathering, and at our backs the shelter of a mighty cedar. As if that was not enough, the clouds lifted, and for a moment, before darkness fell, the great bulk of Hathi Parbat, the 'Elephant Mountain', loomed up across the valley, and far to the northwest the shapely white cone of Nilkanta seemed to stand alone in a darkening sky.

Next day we reached Joshimath, a day in advance of the time appointed for the Mana men. Of these there was no sign—and the telegraph line to Badrinath was broken.

CHAPTER V

THE RISHI GORGE AND BACK AGAIN

◆

JOSHIMATH IS A VILLAGE of some importance on the Pilgrim Road
to Badrinath and two marches short of that place. It is 6000 ft.
above sea level and 1500 ft. above the confluence of the Alaknanda
and Dhauli rivers. At the junction is the temple, so often seen at the
place where two rivers meet, built on a tongue of rock between the
two. This is known as the 'prayag', and the shrine and the few huts
are called Vishnuprayag. There are five such 'prayags' at the five sacred
confluences of the Alaknanda. The river here, and for a few miles up, is
called the Vishnuganga. A flight of stone steps leads down to the water,
which is cold, swift, and deep, and in it the pilgrims bathe ceremonially, hanging to chains and ringbolts to avoid being carried away. Even
with this precaution several lives are said to be lost every year. The long
zigzag path from Vishnuprayag to Joshimath is cut into steps faced
with stones.

The temple, or rather collection of temples, is built round a courtyard and is of great antiquity. Some of them are in a state of dilapi-
dation owing, it is said, to an earthquake, but the temples of Vishnu,
Ganesh, the Sun, Navadevi, and Narsinha are in fair preservation.

The idol of Vishnu is of black stone, well carved, and about seven
feet high. That of Narsinha is reputed to have an arm which dimin-
ishes daily, and when it falls off the road to Badrinath will be closed
by a landslip and a new temple will be erected at Tapoban, seven
miles up the Dhauli valley from Joshimath. The legend giving rise to
this forecast is that Vishnu, in his man-lion incarnation of Narsinha,
visited the palace of an early Raja of this region and asked the wife
of the absent prince for food. Having partaken he lay down on the
bed of the Raja, who found him there on his return from the chase
and struck him on the arm with his sword. Instead of blood, milk
flowed from the wound, and the startled Raja, sensing that he must
have struck a god, asked that his crime might be punished. The deity

disclosed himself, and having ordained that the Raja must leave the pleasant vale of Joshimath, added: 'Remember that this wound which thou hast given me shall also be seen on the image in thy temple, and when that image shall fall to pieces and the hand shall no more remain, thy house shall fall to ruin and thy dynasty shall disappear from amongst the princes of the world.' In one of the Hindu writings is the following:

> The road to Badri never will be closed
> The while at Joshimath Vishnu doth remain;
> But straightway when the god shall cease to dwell,
> The path to Badri will be shut to men.

There is a dak bungalow at Joshimath for the use of travellers and the Rawal of Badrinath has a large house here in which he resides during the winter months. The streets are paved with stone flags and the houses are neatly built with squared stone and roofed with shingles or heavy slates; they are usually of two stories, the ground floor being devoted to a store or shop while the family live above. Traders, cultivators, and temple officials make up the population of about five hundred.

There are two bazaars, where all native foods can be bought; the Sherpas at last got all the atta they wanted and we were able to replenish our stock of sugar, rice, and lentils, and make ourselves sick on the local sweetmeats, which are very good indeed. There were far too many flies about for the fastidious, but, in Garhwal, if you eat only what the flies have not touched then you go hungry. The flies are no doubt worse in Joshimath and along the Pilgrim Road generally, but it would not be right to ascribe this wholly to the pilgrims and their small regard for sanitary rules. All the villages of Garhwal, even up to 7000 and 8000 ft., are plagued with flies, but as a good part of the Pilgrim Road lies in a comparatively low and hot valley they are naturally more numerous in villages on the Road. Chamoli, for example, twenty-five miles below Joshimath, is only 3000 ft. above the sea.

Malaria, dysentry, and cholera, though not exactly rife, are nevertheless prevalent along this Road in the summer. A great deal has been done by the Government to combat this by piping down a clean water supply to the villages, enforcing sanitary rules, and placing a Medical Officer in charge of the Road. Cholera was active in Joshimath and neighbouring villages when we returned there a fortnight later and the Medical Officer, who was then in Joshimath, told us how difficult it was to control, particularly in the outlying and more inaccessible villages to which it sometimes spreads. Bodies are left unburied by the banks of streams which carry infection to lower villages, and the terrified inhabitants migrate, panic-stricken, to other places, taking the infection with them. Corpses are left to rot in the houses and the sick lie untended.

The pilgrim season was in full swing and Joshimath was alive with devotees of all ages and all classes, men and women, rich and poor. To an outsider their demeanour gave the impression that this pilgrimage was more of a disagreeable duty than a pleasure, that the toil and hardships of the road were supported with resignation rather than accepted joyfully as a means of grace—incidents on the road to heaven. But this downcast air may rightly be attributed to the awe and terror which most must feel in the presence of such strange and prodigious manifestations of the power of the gods. Savage crags, roaring torrents, rockbound valleys, hillsides scarred and gashed with terrific landslides, and beyond all the stern and implacable snows—all these must be overwhelming to men whose lives have been passed on the smug and fertile plains, by sluggish and placid rivers, with no hill in sight higher than the village dunghill.

Nor is it remarkable that they should attribute the faintness felt in the rarefied air of Badrinath and Kedarnath to the influence of superhuman powers; or believe that the snow wreaths blowing off the Kedarnath peak are the smoke of sacrifice made by one of Siva's favoured followers, or that the snow banner flying on Nanda Devi is from the kitchen of the goddess herself.

The accomplishment of such a journey by such men must be a tremendous fact in their lives, something to remember when all else has faded. To reach the temple alone is a sign of divine favour, for the gods turn back those with whom they are displeased. The daily exercise, the months of frugal living, the hill air, the sacrifice of time and money, all these must play no small part in the moral and physical regeneration of the pilgrims; and if this salutary discipline of mind and body were to be enjoyed there would perhaps be the less merit. For the mountaineer, it is to be feared, though he penetrate to the ultimate *sanctum sanctorum* of the gods, there is, like the award of the Garter, 'no damned merit about it'—his enjoyment is too palpable.

By midday of June 6th the telegraph line to Badrinath was working and an exchange of telegrams brought the good news that the porters would be down next day. Meantime our 900 lb. of food was ready, half here and half at another village, so that all was set for a start on the 8th, and only a day had been lost. In the perverse way the weather sometimes has, both of these days spent sitting idle in Joshimath were gloriously fine.

Fourteen men from Mana arrived in the evening, among whom were three who had accompanied us in 1934, and on the 8th we did a short march to Tapoban, where the balance of the food was collected and three more local porters enlisted. One of these men, hailing from Bompa, a village higher up the Dhauli, was an amusing character. His name was Kalu and he had chits from previous expeditions in which he appeared to have distinguished himself by going high on Trisul. He was a shameless cadger with an ingratiating manner, and a habit of placing both palms of his hands together as if in prayer whenever he spoke to you. As a mountaineer he thought no small beer of himself, particularly if the conversation should turn to Trisul as it always did if he was taking part in it, and then he would slap his chest like a gorilla, and cry out in a loud voice what great feats Kalu had performed and what greater he was about to do. For all that he worked so well on this trip that at the end I placed too much faith in him and was let down.

At Tapoban we had a fortunate meeting with two British officers out on a shooting trip, who invited us to use their camping ground and join their mess, an invitation we were not slow to accept, as I knew from previous experience that on these shooting trips the doctrine of 'living on the country' is not carried to extreme lengths. But for this chance meeting and the existence of a hot spring, Tapoban would have left nothing but evil memories. The flies were unusually fierce, and as soon as they stopped work at dusk the midges began, and at dawn the reverse process took place.

The hot spring I mentioned is up a little side valley a couple of hundred yards from the road. There is a stone tank about ten feet square and three feet deep, into which gushes a stream of water at a

In the Gorge

temperature of about 90 degrees. The water is clear and sparkling, and has no taste. Close by is a shrine and a hut for its guardian, an emaciated hermit whose hair reached almost to the ground. On this occasion he was absent and we could lie in the bath at ease, increasing the pleasure by running a few yards to a brook where the water was as cold as the bath was hot, and smelt deliciously of wild mint.

A more detailed description of our route may be left for the moment; sufficient to say that after one more vile night of midges in the warm valley we began the climb to the 14,000 ft. pass where flies and midges ceased from troubling. On our way up we met a flock of sheep, and the shepherd was understood to say that one of his sheep had fallen over a cliff and it was ours for the carrying. The Mana men soon found it, skinned it, and went on their way rejoicing; it certainly looked fresh enough, but there was suspiciously little sign of it having suffered a fall. In camp that night when Loomis and I had, after some argument, come to a decision about the respective merits of grilled chops and boiled neck, the inquest was resumed, and we were calmly informed that the sheep had died through eating a poisonous plant. Somehow or other mutton chops ceased to allure and we generously gave our share to the Sherpas. I should hesitate to accuse them of using this stratagem to bring about such a desirable result, but they showed no reluctance to accept fortune's gift and suffered not the slightest ill-effect.

We crossed the pass, now clear of snow, and got down to the Durashi grazing alp. There were no sheep there and we had the place to ourselves, the Mana men finding shelter in some caves, ourselves under the tarpaulin, and the Sherpas in a stone hut used by shepherds. It required a certain lack of imagination to sleep in this hut, because the roof of enormously heavy stones was only supported by some singularly inadequate pieces of wood, one of which was already cracked.

We woke to a wet morning and did not leave till nine o'clock, though this was not much later than usual, for the Mana men are very independent and dislike being hurried. After a leisurely breakfast, the pipe (they had only one) would be passed round several times before they even thought of hinting at a readiness to begin packing up, and unless there was some urgent reason for an early start it was useless to try and hurry them. It was the same on the march; they knew how far they were going and took their own time getting there, sitting down whenever they felt the need for a pipe, which was frequently, and remaining there till all had smoked enough.

The pipe has a ritual of its own: it is a water pipe with a stem about two feet long which is carried by one man; another carries the bowl, a clay affair the size of a jam dish; the bamboo mouthpiece, also two feet long, is carried by a third, the tobacco by a fourth, and the flint and steel by a fifth. If there is any straggling on the march it is some time before the whole is assembled and yet longer before the thing is fairly alight; unless there happens to be a fire handy, when they simply put a burning brand on top of the bowl and leave it there. These dilatory habits are somewhat exasperating, but the men are withal so active and sturdy and reliable that it is impossible to find fault, and if a special effort is required they can and will move quicker than most. Nor is there ever any trouble about making up their loads and deciding who will carry what, a blessing which only those who have travelled with African porters can really appreciate. In their case this unenviable task of apportioning loads usually begins with a free fight and ends with the abandonment of the heaviest load.

Between Durashi and the lower grazing alp of Dibrugheta lies an easy grass pass involving an ascent of 1000 ft. from Durashi and a descent of 3000 ft. to Dibrugheta. The ridge which is crossed by this pass was, by Dr Longstaff, aptly named 'The Curtain'; away from the pass towards the Rishi the ridge rises and the grass slope changes to enormous slabs of smooth, grey rock, which jut right out to the river and completely hide the lower part of the gorge, like the fire curtain on some vast stage.

We sat for some time on the ridge waiting in vain for a view up the gorge to Nanda Devi. Then the Mana men, having had their smoke, took it into their heads to build two enormous cairns and to dedicate them to Loomis and myself, first asking our names, which the scholar amongst them then wrote in Urdu on a stone with a piece of charcoal. This cairn building and stone balancing is the national pastime amongst Tibetans and kindred people such as Sherpas, who are likewise Bhuddists, and these Bhotias who, though nominally Hindus, possibly came from Tibet originally and have maintained a connection with that country ever since. They will run up a noble cairn out of the most unlikely material in a very short time, and crown the whole with stones of diminishing size, skilfully balanced, one on top of the other.

Meanwhile it had started raining again, but the cairns had to be finished off, and in no slovenly manner either, before we were allowed to go on. Rain on the march was to be particularly dreaded at this time, because although the flour and rice were put up in Willesden canvas bags these would not stand a prolonged soaking, and the food was going to be left for six weeks or more before being eaten.

At Dibrugheta we were once more down among birch and pine forest and the Mana men made themselves elaborate huts roofed with birch bark. This invaluable material has many uses. We have all heard of birch-bark canoes, here we were using it for thatching, and it was strongly recommended to me by a former traveller in these parts as a substitute for tobacco, though after trying it I decided that this was a joke in rather bad taste. The Mana men were full of beans this evening, and when they had finished their meal the lads amongst them started throwing lighted brands on the roof of each other's huts, and the whole mob roared with delight when someone's hut was burnt down.

The next camp beyond Dibrugheta is the Cave Camp and here all hands can be accommodated in caves. That is true at least of a party of reasonable size such as ours was then, but it puzzled us to know what we should do when the main body of fifty or more came, because of tent sites there were none. Loomis and I slept that night on a mattress of bags of food to escape the adamantine hardness of the cave floor.

We made the first small food dump here where it was dry, and where it was beyond the reach of those in the villages who might be curious to know what we had done with so much food. It was now the 13th and it was time to think of turning back. But things were going well, the farther we got the food the better, and above all I wanted to have a look at the difficult part of the gorge to see if the route would still 'go'. It was conceivable that since 1934 a fall of rock or the disappearance of some grass or trees from the cliff faces would have made the gorge impassable. One of the charms of the route then discovered was the weakness of some of the links in it and the absence of any alternatives. We therefore decided to go on for another three days, long enough to take us beyond all difficulties and to the threshold of the Promised Land.

The Slabs

Our march that day took us to what had been our base camp in 1934, a pleasant camp under a big rock overhang on the south side of the Rishi Ganga, which can be crossed here by a natural bridge. Before dropping down to the crossing of the Rishi, the glacier-fed torrent of the Rhamani, coming down from the north, had to be crossed. At this time of year it was not a serious obstacle, but for all that it was no place to cross without the support of the third leg which an ice-axe provides. Accordingly as soon as I had crossed, instead of waiting for the rope, I foolishly threw my axe back for Loomis, whose own axe, it will be remembered, had been lost. The bank on that side was steep and high and, instead of landing on top, the axe hit a boulder and bounced back into the river. Loomis made one unavailing grab and then jumped into the river after it, and the net result of two pieces of foolishness was the loss of his topee and my ice-axe.

After carrying an axe for some days one feels lost at first without it, but in the Rishi, where it is better to have both hands available rather than one hand and an axe, it was really more of a hindrance than a help. The loss of the topee might have been serious for anyone with a sensitive skull, but none of us found such things necessary in Garhwal, which is outside the tropics and in about the same latitude as Cairo.

The natural bridge over the Rishi, which is formed by an enormous boulder, caused some delay. All loads had to be lowered down to it and on the boulder itself a rope was necessary because the branches, which in 1934 we had placed there as ladders, had all gone. However, all got safely over and there we were only two days from the Basin, with ten loads of food, and a dry overhang under which to sleep.

From this point the way lies straight up the south wall of the gorge to a height of about 1500 ft. above the river, and from there pursues a horizontal or slightly downwards course—what we call a traverse. The first 400 or 500 ft. out of the river bed are steep and exposed, and the climber is disquietingly dependent on branches of trees and tufts of grass for his safety. No further difficulty is encountered until the beginning of the traverse. From a grass terrace a rock chimney leads up to what we called the 'Slabs', smooth rock sloping upwards at such an angle that with a load on it is difficult to stand up with any confidence. These slabs form the floor of a wide gully, which just below here plunges down to the Rishi at a much steeper angle. Above the slabs is a rock wall which can be climbed on the left by men without loads, and these can then be hauled directly up the wall.

We arrived at this place and found the slabs dry, and Loomis and I, who were in rubbers and had only moderate loads, got up without a rope. The Mana men go barefoot and most of them climb like cats, but here only a few of them, and neither of the Sherpas, despised the aid of the rope. Loads were dumped and some of us climbed to the top of the wall and began hauling while the others remained below to tie on. It is a slow job at the best, and I climbed down again to hasten matters, as I wanted to get finished before the rain started; we had a rope 120 ft. long so that both ends could be used—tying a load on one end while the other was being hauled up. To superintend this I was standing on a narrow ledge about twenty feet above the floor of the gully and, thick-headedly enough, almost under the rope. Things then happened quickly. Gazing at an ascending load I was petrified to see a large flake of rock, probably loosened by the rope, sliding down the wall straight for me. Whether it hit me, or whether I stepped back to avoid it, is only of academic interest because the result was the same, and next instant I was falling twenty feet on to the slabs, head first and face to the wall, for I distinctly remember seeing it go past. Hitting the slabs I rolled for a bit and then luckily came to rest before completing the 1400 odd feet into the river.

In a minute or two I was able to sit up and take notice, and having told the load-haulers to get on with it, crawled up the slabs to a more secure place and assessed the damage. A sprained shoulder and thumb, a bruised thigh and a cracked rib, and a lot of skin missing was the sum total. None were serious, and it might have been much worse; in which case, I thought, the last lines of a little verse about the man who tried to hurry the East would not have been inapplicable: 'And the end of the fight is a tombstone white with the name of the late deceased, And this epitaph drear, "A fool lies here who tried to hurry the East."'

It was necessary to get moving before stiffness made this impossible, so with a rope on and some men shoving behind, I was got up to the top of the wall, and when the loads were all up we started for Half-way Camp, which was still a mile distant.

Next day Loomis went on with the men and dumped all the remaining loads at Pisgah Camp within sight of the Sanctuary, and

64   THE ASCENT OF NANDA DEVI

returned the same day to Halfway Camp. I lay in camp and felt sorry
for myself, wondering how I was to get back, for the slightest movement was difficult, to-morrow was the 17th, and we were due in Ranikhet on the 25th.

With Pasang Kikuli assisting I started very early next morning, in
advance of the others, who caught us up at the 'Slabs'. These were difficult for me because both arms were useless, but the Mana men were
very solicitous and skilful and before midday we reached the overhang
by the Rishi. After an hour's rest we pushed on over the bridge, which
had now been made easier by placing trees there, and Cave Camp was
reached the same day.

Another double march followed, Kalu and the Mana headman
taking care of me. The 3000 ft. climb up to the 'Curtain' ridge from
Dibrugheta was enlivened by a violent hail storm and we were so per-
ished with cold that, on arrival at Durashi, Loomis and I shared the
stone hut with the Sherpas, caring little whether the roof fell in or not.
Still marching double stages we crossed the pass and got down to flies
and the Dhauli valley next day, and on the 20th reached Joshimath,
not omitting to wallow for an hour in the hot spring at Tapoban in the
hope that it would ease my battered limbs, which, when they realised
they were not likely to get any rest, began to respond to this 'healing
by faith' treatment.

Here we paid off the Mana men, giving them a liberal tip at which
they grumbled loudly for, unlike the Sherpas who do this sort of work
more for its own sake than for the money, they are out for all they can
get and value their services highly. For all their complaining, they let
it be understood that they would be willing to come with us again
next month, despite our illiberal notions about baksheesh. Kalu had
already engaged himself, and had undertaken the collection of another
ten loads of coolie food, assuring me that I could rely on him to have it
ready waiting for us, an assurance I was foolish enough to accept.

Now that the Mana men had gone, Loomis and I had no one to
carry our loads, and for me it was painful enough to get along at all,
without having to carry a load. We combed the bazaar for a coolie,
but at ten o'clock gave it up and left in pouring rain and in a very
sour mood. It was late that evening before we camped amongst the
pines not far below our old camp site. On the 22nd we crossed the

Kuari, went on through Kaliaghat and down to the Bireh Ganga. The bridge was down but a repair gang were at work on it and, after a short wait, two logs were got into a sufficiently stable position to cross with the aid of a rope. Spray was dashing over the logs and Pasang Phuta was rash enough to try it in rubber shoes, slipped on the wet wood, and hung suspended with his load in the water and his head not far off it. He was soon rescued from this undignified and perilous position and we pushed on and camped in the gathering dark some way above the river.

We seemed to be getting into a defiant sort of mood and evinced a growing determination to reach Ranikhet in five days from Joshimath, cost what effort it might. Next day we crossed the ridge, got down to the Ramni bungalow at midday and, encouraged by hearing that the bridge on the direct route was repaired, crossed the Nandakini and trudged the 2000 ft. up to Kanol, camping at six o'clock in a field.

I was rapidly recovering under this treatment, but Loomis was not well; yet on the following day we eclipsed all previous efforts and covered what are normally three stages, reaching the Gwaldam bungalow at half-past seven at night. We learnt that the Ranikhet bus left Garul at five in the morning, and we toyed with the idea of leaving Gwaldam again in the small hours to catch it. But in the night there was tremendous rain and it was so jolly sitting once more in a chair with a roof over our heads and a fire at our feet that we consigned this particular bus to the devil and strolled down to Garul like gentlemen late in the forenoon. By paying rather more than the usual fare we persuaded another bus to start and got back to Ranikhet on the evening of the 25th, twenty-eight days after leaving it.

CHAPTER VI

'SCRAPPING AND BAGGING'

———————◆———————

THANKS TO THE GOODWILL of the Forest Service we had been given the use of the Ranikhet Forest Bungalow, and here we installed ourselves to begin work and to await the arrival of the others. It is a big building of eight rooms, with a wide verandah running round two sides which made an ideal place for the reception of the flood of cases which was about to engulf us. Furthermore, it is one of the most pleasantly situated bungalows in Ranikhet and commands a complete panorama of the snows from the Kedarnath peaks in the west to Nepal in the east.

We were told that the weather had been atrocious ever since we left, the monsoon having set in exceptionally early. Comparing notes it seemed that the weather had been less severe where we were, farther north, and personally I did not consider monsoon conditions really established in the north until we returned to Joshimath on the 20th. However, there was no doubt about it then, for it rained all the way back and, except for a short break, continued to rain throughout our stay in Ranikhet; so much so that the later arrivals never got a glimpse of a mountain until we reached the Kuari Pass. During this brief fine spell Loomis and I, and Arthur Emmons, the second of the American contingent to arrive, had some clear views of the Range. The side of Nanda Devi which can be seen from Ranikhet is that by which our attempt was to be made, and after studying it through glasses and telescope we could only express a pious hope that it was not so bad as it looked.

Emmons, who joined us on the 28th, had done some climbing in Alaska and was one of the party which in 1932 climbed Minya Gonkar (24,900 ft.), a peak in the south-west of China near the Tibet border. While at the highest camp on this mountain Emmons had been severely frost-bitten in both feet, which he was fortunate not to lose altogether. He was still able to climb, in fact he had since been to the Alps; but he

66

was not able to go high because frost-bite is very apt to recur in a limb which has already been attacked. He was to take charge of the base for us and carry out a survey.

Most of the food and equipment had now arrived, and although a considerable quantity of food was purposely left at Delhi, we yet had far more than we could use, due mainly to preparations having been made on a Kangchenjunga scale for a party of twelve. This was not such a happy position as it may sound. Some stoicism was required for the scrapping of so much good food, and even with only three present whose tastes need be considered, it was hard to satisfy everyone. It was all the more important therefore to get this job done before any other members of the party arrived, further to darken counsel by urging the claims of their pet foods.

Without wishing to appear overrighteous I may say that I was indifferent to what we took so long as it was food and not chemicals, and gave value for weight. That this attitude involved no self-sacrifice I might add that in my opinion all tinned foods tasted the same, and that if we had to take a hundred pounds of tinned meat the propor-tion of ham, tongue, chicken, roast beef, bully beef, or even sardines was of no consequence. And the same might be said of cereals, of which we had a weird and wonderful assortment of every hue and texture, but which in the end all boiled down to porridge. Tinned jams too are more distinguishable by colour than by taste and, when these came up for selection, I put in a mild plea on behalf of honey to the exclusion of all jam, a plea which received more favourable hearing because its advocate had taken no part in the fierce contests which raged over, say, oatmeal versus hominy grits, and corned beef against roast beef. Having fixed the total weight of food required and deducted what I considered the essentials, namely all the pem-mican, cheese, biscuit, and, if possible, honey, that we had with us, plus sugar at the rate of half a pound a day a man, the remaining weight was then apportioned between meat, cereals, sweet-stuffs, and miscellaneous, and Loomis and Emmons filled the lists in detail, toss-ing up, presumably, for first pick. The method might not have been approved by a dietitian, but the results were satisfactory and nobody groused about the food, at least not until circumstance compelled us to jettison a lot more.

Saving weight was to my mind all-important, and this doctrine found ready backers amongst the others, especially those who had climbed in Alaska or British Columbia, where porters as understood in the Himalaya are non-existent, and everything has to be carried on the climber's back. When porters are available, as in this case, it may seem immaterial whether we took forty or fifty, apart from the small extra cost. But the route up the Rishi is difficult for heavily laden porters and a slip might have serious consequences, so that every coolie in excess of the minimum was an added responsibility. It was not like climbing on a mountain with a few Sherpas, when Europeans are roped to the porters and able to look after them. Roping together large numbers is not very practicable nor can you festoon three miles of cliff with fixed ropes, and in most of the places where a slip might occur no safeguards are possible.

When a large amount of tinned food is taken the packing is no small proportion of the total weight. For example, 30 lb. of bully beef packed in 1 lb. tins, or sometimes ½ lb. tins, weighs nearly 40 lb.; it is seldom safe to allow less than one-fifth of the total for packing, and more often it is a fourth. We saved what weight we could by bulking where possible, and things like cereals and dried fruits were put in waterproof bags. In only one instance did our zeal for saving weight outrun discretion, when a certain much-advertised drink in powder form was put in bags and promptly coagulated into a stiff, glutinous mass. To some of us it was more palatable in this toffee form than as a drink.

When the remainder of the party arrived, the results and implications of this scrap and bag policy were regarded with mixed feelings. 'Scrapping and bagging' became a stock jest and dark hints were thrown out that the leader of the 'scrap and bag' school should himself be scrapped, or at any rate bagged. It was a job for a Fisher and I am afraid that unlike him none of us were sufficiently 'ruthless, and remorseless'.

The weight suggested for our personal gear, including sleeping bag and boots, was 35 lb. Boots were included among gear to be carried, because for the approach march everyone used the highly unorthodox footwear of rubber shoes, usually without socks too, until beyond Joshimath, and some of the more impious wore them on to the

W. F. Loomis, Charles Houston, N. E. Odell, Adams Carter (at back),
H. W. Tilman, T. Graham Brown, Peter Lloyd, A. B. Emmons

Pasang Phuta, Kitar, Nuri, Pasang Kikuli, Nima Tsering, Kalu
Both taken at Base Camp, August 9th

glacier. If the weight was kept down to this poundage per person each Sherpa could carry his own kit of 25 lb. and his Sahib's, and the Sahibs would march unladen, at least as far as Joshimath. In practice this was unsatisfactory, for most people then proceeded to burden themselves with a private rucksack and another 20 lb. or more of personal belongings. Very little of this extra stuff was used, but was dumped at various places from Tapoban onwards and later solemnly carried back again. It is rather a problem deciding what you must take and what you can leave behind, but it is amazingly simplified when you know that you have to carry it all yourself.

The Sherpas' personal effects wanted a lot of overhauling to keep them within the stipulated weight, and in their case it was possible to be dictatorial. But, despite the severest scrutiny, when we arrived in the Basin one of them suddenly appeared wearing a wholly unauthorised and very unexpeditionary pair of trousers, another a favourite pair of buttoned boots.

To conclude this overlong dissertation on weight, I should add that on the day before starting, when most of the others were out or too preoccupied, Charles Houston and I had a glorious hour amongst the 'kitchen' and 'miscellaneous junk' loads, which resulted in the scrapping of most of the innumerable articles included for the time-honoured reason that 'they might come in useful', and the reduction of our eating utensils to a mug and a spoon apiece.

The four additional Sherpas arrived on July 3rd. One of them, Nuri, had been with me in Sikkim, two I had looked at in Darjeeling and turned down on the score of age. These were Da Namgyal and Nima Tsering, who were both on Everest in 1924 but who now seemed, from one cause or another, to be past any really strenuous work, as indeed the event proved. The fourth was Kitar, who had an extraordinary record of expeditionary work to his credit but who did not seem to us a very likeable type of Sherpa. He had been on the Everest expeditions of 1922, 1924, and 1933, Kangchenjunga expeditions of 1929, 1930, 1931, and Nanga Parbat of 1934 when he, Pasang Kikuli, and three others were the only survivors of the eleven high-camp porters.

The remainder of the party, excepting Odell, arrived on July 6th and included Graham Brown, Peter Lloyd, and Charles Houston. The last named was the third American, and had organised the attempt on Mount Foraker in which Graham Brown had taken part. Odell, in the tradition of learned professors, was last, and we were still one American short. This was Adams Carter, who on this particular date was believed to be in Shanghai, rather a long way from Nanda Devi. Apparently there had been some misunderstanding, and he was under the impression that we were not going to tackle the mountain until after the monsoon. I thought it would be hardly worth his while to come, but in this I reckoned without his resource or the possibilities of air travel. Anyhow, we sent him a cable to the effect that we were starting on the 10th, and that if he could not reach Ranikhet within a fortnight of that date, he might as well stay in Shanghai.

Odell, who was intending to do a lot of geological work, and who as a scientist lent seriousness to our otherwise frivolous proceedings, had gone to Simla and was not to arrive until the 8th. This was a source of worry to me, who had to arrange the transport, for it was credibly reported that he was accompanied by a mountain of luggage, would probably acquire more scientific instruments in Simla, while others of the same genus were said to be converging on Ranikhet from various parts of Europe and America. Meantime we had to tell the coolie agent with whom we were dealing exactly how many coolies we required, for these Dotial porters have to be sent for from some distance and would have to start in advance of us. Making a guess, I mentally devoted two coolies to the service of science, and prayed fervently that the reports were exaggerated and that the instruments on the way would arrive too late; as happily they did.

The Dotial porters do not come from Garhwal but from Doti, a corner of Nepal bordering on the Almora district, which perhaps accounts for some of their toughness. They are a class of professional porters and most of the carrying in Garhwal is done by them: an exception to this is on the Pilgrim Road, where the men who carry the dandies all come from the native state of Tehri Garhwal. They are very strong and the normal load for a Dotial on a good road is 80 lb.

In 1934 Shipton and I employed eleven Dotials to carry from Ranikhet to the entrance of the gorge, and, when eight coolies from the Dhauli villages deserted, these men stood by us, added all but two of the abandoned loads to their own, and carried 80 lb. over the 14,000 ft.

pass when it was still deep in snow. Their behaviour then had left me with a very high opinion of their qualities, and though, on that occasion, we did not take them over the most difficult part of the gorge, I was confident of their ability to tackle it.

Yet there was a risk in relying entirely on them, because amongst the large number we proposed taking there were likely to be some who were not equal to difficult climbing, and coming, as they do, from a comparatively low, hot country the cold and wet conditions we expected to encounter in the gorge might knock all the stuffing out of them. The Mana men, on the other hand, could climb anything and were pretty well impervious to weather, the result of living part of the year at 10,000 ft. and most of it at yet higher altitudes tending their flocks. But on the last trip they had told me that we could not get forty Bhotias because not many would be willing to come on an engagement of only three weeks' duration, being at this season more profitably employed trading with Tibet. I therefore decided to rely mainly on Dotials and to leaven the lump with a few Mana men.

For this purpose thirty-seven Dotials paraded in the bazaar on July 7th and, having been signed on and given an advance of pay, were instructed to meet us at Garul on July 10th. Two of these were of the gallant eleven of 1934, and one, Aujra, appointed himself as headman, but on the understanding that he would carry a load. The aid of my friend the Rawal of Badrinath was again invoked, and I asked him to send ten Mana men to meet us in Joshimath on the 19th.

But for this man Aujra we employed no headman, cooks, or other idlers, but each Sahib had a Sherpa allotted to him as servant. There were seven of us, and only six Sherpas, so Pasang Kikuli was detailed to look after Graham Brown and myself while the others had each a Sherpa. This was not so unselfish as it appears, because Pasang could and did attend to the needs of two better than his fellows could look after one, doing most of the camp work into the bargain. Da Namgyal was told off for Odell and proved to be the perfect 'gentleman's gentleman'; and this was most fitting because Odell was the only one amongst us capable of doing his man credit and of upholding the white man's prestige. By talking to Da Namgyal very loudly and clearly in English, Odell at once arrived at a complete understanding, and thenceforward he was attended by a perfect valet who, with a little encouragement, would have pressed his master's shorts and polished the nails of his climbing boots.

To Da Namgyal the rest of us were rather low and common, scarcely Sahibs in fact; the Americans, especially at first, were rather impatient of too much attention, and I must say it is a bit corrupting to have your boots put on and your pipe lit for you. However, I noticed that before long they acquiesced not unwillingly in the ways of the country and were as ready as the rest of us to shout 'koi hai' on the slightest pretext.*

Nima Tsering, who was large and tough-looking, was given to Loomis who was even larger, so that if necessary he could be repressed. He turned out to be our second best man in spite of his age and the effects, as they told me in Darjeeling, of a life-long belief that 'beer is best'. Fortunately, or unfortunately from some points of view, Garhwal is 'dry', at least I have never, or seldom, come across any beer in the villages, though that might be because the search was not diligent enough. Had it been there I am sure the Sherpas would have found it, but we never had any trouble from them on this account. Nima was as strong as a horse and very ready and active, with a prodigious grin in front and a magnificent pigtail behind. He was the only one of our six to wear a pigtail, and I confess to being prejudiced in favour of Sherpas who do wear one if only because it may mean that they have not been enervated by long residence in Darjeeling.

Pasang Phuta, who, as I have remarked, was a bit bovine, and Nuri, who was small and frail, were allotted to Lloyd and Houston respectively because they seemed least in need of assistance. Emmons took Kitar because he was not travelling with the main body, but was riding to Joshimath by the Pilgrim Road to save his feet and needed someone reliable with him. Kitar knew the ropes, having been to Garhwal some years ago with Mr Ruttledge and again, only a month previously, with an Austrian traveller.

All was now set for a start. On the evening of the 9th two lorries came up to the bungalow and were loaded with our 2500 lb. of stuff to facilitate an early start next morning. To save weight nearly all the loads were packed in gunny bags instead of boxes. These served the

* 'Koi hai' means 'anyone there?'—the usual way of calling a servant.

purpose well enough and managed to last out the wear and tear of a rough journey; the only disadvantage was that when anything was wanted they had first to be unstitched and then sewn up again: we carried a supply of twine and packing needles. It speaks well for the honesty of our men that although very little was under lock and key nothing was stolen.

A mass of surplus kit and equipment was now carried over to a neighbouring bungalow and stored there against our return. For this and many other kindnesses we were indebted to Mrs Browne, an old resident of Ranikhet, who has travelled extensively in Garhwal and as far as Tibet. Carter's kit and a small tent were left here ready for him should he arrive, and Mrs Browne undertook to take charge of him and see him started on the road to Joshimath. It had rained without pause for the last forty-eight hours and next morning, when we piled ourselves and the Sherpas into the lorries, it looked like continuing for another forty-eight. No one was there to see us off—a few words of chaff passed with Emmons—and so we started with hopes which no rain could quench.

CHAPTER VII

THE FOOTHILLS

◆

THE FIFTY MILES OF ROAD between Ranikhet and Garul are carved for the most part out of abrupt hill sides and are as full of kinks as a wriggling eel. The heavy rain had started many small landslips, and rounding every one of the innumerable bends I half expected to find the road completely blocked. Nor was it comforting to reflect that only yesterday a lorry from Kathgodam had slipped off the road and gone down the *khud* with fatal results. Such gloomy thoughts must have been roused by a too early and too heavy breakfast, and it was with a feeling of having been delivered from a great peril that I got down at Garul at midday.

Our thirty-seven Dotials were all present and correct, one or two capitalists sheltering under battered umbrellas, for it continued to rain cheerfully. The thirty-seven loads were dumped in the mud and presently these were adjusted to the satisfaction of all, the headman, having successfully palmed off most of his on to the more complacent of his followers, contenting himself with an umbrella and a canvas bucket, perhaps with a view to being prepared for both contingencies—flood or drought. There was some talk of stopping for the night at a dak bungalow two miles away, the headman arguing with some cogency that it was raining (a fact which might have escaped our notice) and quoting the time-honoured rule that the first day's march should be a short one. To this I replied that if we only marched in fine weather we should not march at all, that they had already marched for two days from Ranikhet so that it was not their first day, and as for ourselves, though it was kind of him to think of us, we would for once make an exception to the rule.

Gwaldam was therefore our destination, ten miles away and a long climb, and it must have been a portentous sight for the Garulians to see this long caravan sliding and slipping out of their muddy village, most of us brandishing an ice-axe in one hand and an umbrella in the other, some draped in green oilskin cycling capes, and one even crowned with a sou'wester. I remembered the march to Gwaldam in 1934 as a decidedly grim affair, for it was a grilling hot day in May, and when we finally crawled into the bungalow we were more dead than alive. To-day nobody seemed to feel it much, not even those who had only recently stepped off a ship, and the slowest of the porters was in by half-past six. There is much to be said for travelling in the monsoon.

The Gwaldam bungalow is a poor place, at least for a party of six; its best feature is the magnificent view which of course we were not to see, save only for a patch of snow which, through a break in the clouds, appeared for a moment high up and seemingly belonged to no earthly mountain. Nor were we more favoured with material things; the usual inquiry for eggs and milk met with the usual reply.

The Dotials had been asking questions about the route, and, hearing that the bridge over the Nandakini was again down, had mapped out a new route for us some distance to the west of the more usual way. Accordingly next morning, when we dropped down through a forest of noble 'chir' trees (*Pinus longifolia*) to the Pindar river, instead of crossing it, we turned west and marched down the valley to a place called Tharali. Here the river was crossed by a wire suspension bridge and the camping ground, a green flat on the river bank, was pointed out to us. It was too public and looked too wet to be very inviting, and since the march had been but short we asked if there was nothing better ahead. There is only one answer to such a question, even should there happen to be a stream round the next corner, and we were hastily assured that there was no water for at least ten miles. For once the liars who told us this did us an inestimable service, for, in consequence of believing them and stopping there, we got three dozen eggs on the spot and two dozen more next morning. Blessings on Tharali! And the more pity that it should have been singled out for vengeance by the flooding of the Pindar river. No doubt the more pious Garhwali considered that Tharali was doubly damned and deserved all it got, not only for keeping the unclean hen but, worse still, for selling the product to the defilers of the shrine of the Blessed Goddess.

The camping-ground belied its wet appearance, the sun shone for a brief interval, we broached a 10 lb. cheese of perfect maturity, bathed

Camp between Tharali and Ghat

in the icy Pindar, and were the subject of much amiable curiosity on the part of young Tharali.

It rained again at night and in the early morning, but we got away in good time, for it was advisable to inculcate good habits while the expedition was in its infancy. The usual routine was for me to get up about five and rout out the Sherpas, or rather two of them, for the others seldom came to life until much later. Nima was very good and was generally out first to light the fire, with Pasang Kikuli a close second ready to cook the food I gave him. A great beaker of tea all round was the first thing and then, while the porridge was cooking, Pasang and I started making the chapatties. Pasang was an artist at this and what is more he always washed his hands before getting to work. The mathematically perfect circles of thin dough which he cleverly slapped down on to the hot plate were the envy and despair of all who tried their hands at this game of skill. The amateur's effort was of any shape, varying from an ellipse to something resembling the map of England, that is if it ever reached such an advanced stage; more often it was beaten to fragments or slipped out of the hands on to the ground before ever it was ready for the neat backhander which should, but seldom did, spread it flat on the iron plate. The beaker of tea and the noise we made whacking away at chapatties were the signal for the others to 'rise and shine', though precious little 'shining' was done after the first few days.

When our breakfast was off the fire the Sherpas started cooking theirs—at this stage of the journey usually a vast mountain of rice and a mouth-blistering sauce containing 100 per cent. chillies to help it down. Some might have preferred the breakfast order reversed, Sherpas first and Sahibs last, but as it was we had a pleasant interval for digestion, smoking a pipe, writing up diaries, or any other odd job before having to pack up and march.

To-day we turned north up a pleasant side valley through more pine forest, and then west again, heading for a gap in the ridge. Camp was made on a delightful green terrace set amidst oak trees, three miles beyond the last village and 8000 ft. up. Odell and I were in first, and while waiting for the porters we stripped and walked back down the road to a nearby waterfall for a bathe. Odell was out of luck; he was surprised by a bevy of ancient beldames and was forced to flee in confusion pursued by a volley of Garhwali Billingsgate.

It began to rain as the porters arrived and all our seven tents had to be pitched for their accommodation. We slept three in a tent, the Sherpas five, the Dotials seven, and those who were left over sought shelter in some shepherds' huts close by. One function of a tent is to keep out rain, but we were now beginning to suspect that the makers of our tents were not aware of this. Every seam dripped, and, where the guys joined the fabric, rivers flowed out to collect on the floor into young lakes, which were summarily dealt with by stabbing a hole in the ground-sheet with a knife. These tents were not made in America, but poor Houston, who was responsible for them and who, under the sheltering roof of the forest bungalow, had waxed eloquent over the impeccable behaviour of the same type in Alaska, came in for some merciless chaff. 'Were they equally good in snow?' we asked, 'and was the rain in Alaska very dry?' And an insect common in Garhwal, though hitherto unknown to science, was discovered for Houston's benefit—a flying leech, which we assured him would fly through these precious tents as easily as the drops of rain.

The mention of insects constrains me to add the following. The seven tents were in two sizes, 6 ft. x 7 ft. and 7 ft. x 8 ft., but in appearance all were alike and now, having given them out to the Dotials, I suddenly called to mind a little roadside incident I had witnessed only that morning. Two Dotials were resting by the wayside, one of them subjecting an indescribably dirty shirt to a close scrutiny, while his companion, sitting behind, did a like office for his head. I kept this disturbing memory to myself and there and then went out, armed with an indelible pencil, and marked with a large 'S' the tents used by ourselves and the Sherpas.

While on the subject of tents I may say, to anticipate matters, that on the mountain the tents were severely tested and behaved very well.

Next day's march took us down to the Nandakini river, about ten miles down stream of the old route, at a place called Ghat. It was not a long march; indeed the stages on this route seemed to me much easier than those of the other, and the Pindar-Nandakini watershed was crossed at a height of only 8900 ft. instead of 10,000 ft. From the pass we followed a delightful river, in which we bathed, down to its junction with the Nandakini; bathing was rapidly becoming an obsession and we did it again in the Nandakini, across which Houston swam, greatly to the astonishment of the natives.

At Ghat a dak bungalow was in the last stages of construction; there were no doors or windows and the debris which always accumulates during building operations lay thick on the floor—but for all that we occupied it, most of us, even Houston, preferring to be dry though dirty. There was nothing interesting to eat here, and though a man went down to the river at dusk with a net the hopes thus aroused were not fulfilled. Mahseer are found in these bigger rivers where the water is not too cold.

At breakfast next morning we were entertained by a party of strolling minstrels, two bold-looking hussies who sang and an insignificant little man playing a drum with his fingers. We gave them a rupee, which was apparently far too much, for they were quite beside themselves with delight and I feared they would follow us up the mountain.

The Nandakini was crossed by a permanent bridge and for four hours the road zigzagged steadily up a steep slope bare of trees. From the top there was an uninterrupted view up the valley, where the river slowly uncoiled itself like a silver snake between the dark olive green of the forested slopes, flecked with sunshine and shadow. We gazed for a long time, waiting vainly for the great white dome of Trisul to reveal itself at the valley head, while a wandering shepherd beguiled the time for us with the music of his pipe.

The road now contoured the hillside, converging gradually towards the old route and finally joining it in the little village of Ramni, where we took up our quarters in the same ramshackle bungalow.

A Garhwal village is, at any rate from a distance, a very delightful and humanising incident in the Himalayan landscape. It is generally built on a spur or half-way up the slope of a hill, so that the cultivation extends both above and below. Regard must of course be had to the water supply, and this should preferably be from two sources, so that the low-caste Doms shall not foul the water of their betters the Biths (Brahmans and Rajputs). The houses are of stone and are two-storied and in front is a stone court-yard bounded by a low stone wall. It is here that the threshing, winnowing, and weaving are carried on. Fruit trees are sometimes planted round the court-yard, peach trees in the higher valleys and bananas or plantains in the lower.

The village with its solid stone houses, sometimes having the walls white-washed, surrounded by terraced fields, has a very satisfying appearance—an appearance of comfort, warmth, and prosperity that is many times accentuated for the traveller who first views it after many weeks above the tree-line.

It rained during the night, and in the morning we climbed in dank mist through dripping rhododendron forest to the top of the ridge at nearly 11,000 ft. Between Ramni and Kaliaghat, the usual halting-place, is a delightfully situated grazing alp called Shim Kharak. I had pleasant recollections of camping there in 1934, but hearing a report that the bridge over the Bireh Ganga was down, we decided to push on and camp closer to the river, so that we could learn the truth of this report and if necessary begin building operations.

We camped a mile short of the bridge and 500 ft. above the river, and Aujra, the headman, went on down to look at the bridge. He reported that the bridge, a tree-trunk affair, was still standing, but that the river was almost lapping it. This news made us very uneasy; it was fine at the moment, but if it rained in the night the bridge would probably go.

Sure enough it rained all night and was hard at it next morning when we hurried down to the river expecting the worst. From half-way down we caught sight of the river through the trees, and there was the bridge with the water a clear two feet below it. It seemed doubtful whether Aujra had gone to the bridge yesterday or merely drawn on his imagination, but I was too thankful to press the inquiry, and rather felt it was a job one of us ought to have done. Had the bridge gone we should certainly have been held up for a day or more, for it would have been no easy matter to throw fresh logs across the forty feet of rushing water.

Climbing up the north side of the valley we could see where the river widened out into the Gohna Lake, the result of a great landslip which occurred in 1893, damming up the Bireh Ganga until a lake of many square miles was formed. At first reports from the local head-man that a mountain had fallen were ignored, but when the place was visited by Lieut.-Col. Pulford, R.E., Superintending Engineer, it was found that a succession of slips had formed a dam 900 ft. high, 11,000 ft. wide at the base, and 2000 ft. wide at the top. His opinion was that nothing would happen until the water topped the dam and, in spite of other experts holding contrary views, this opinion was adopted and acted upon, and in the event was triumphantly justified.

An engineer was put on to watch the rise of the water and a light telegraph wire erected for the purpose of warning the towns and villages down the Ganges valley. The danger limits of the expected flood were marked out by masonry pillars beyond which the inhabitants were warned to retreat. Suspension bridges were taken down and pilgrim traffic diverted to other routes.

Final calculations predicted that the flood was not to be expected until August 1894, and on August 25th the water began to trickle over the dam and at midnight it collapsed with an appalling crash. The flood lasted until the morning of the 26th, when it was found the lake had fallen 390 ft. Only one life was lost, but much damage was done all down the river, the town of Srinagar being swept away. From the permanent lake which now exists, the water escapes over the sound remains of the huge barrier.

The enormous grey scar on the hillside above gave us but a faint notion of the cataclysmic nature of the event. The steepness of the valleys, the nature of the rock, and the heavy rain combine to make landslips a frequent occurrence and the maintenance of roads a task of Sisyphus.

It was still drizzling when we reached Kaliaghat at midday and camped amongst the giant boulders, the Dotials boldly and, as it chanced, unwisely deciding to use the spare tents instead of walking a mile to the village. After a fine afternoon it began again in earnest that night, and was raining heavier than ever when we got up. Breakfast was cooked under difficulties, or, to be accurate, under an umbrella. When this dismal rite was over, the flood continued unabated and the porters were averse to starting, saying that a river at the foot of the Kauri Pass would be unfordable. They had already abandoned the tents and taken refuge in a derelict cowshed, and since everyone was wet and miserable we made their faintheartedness an excuse for 'lying at earth', as Mr Jorrocks would express it, when the weather was too bad for hunting. This decision cost us Rs 37, a day's pay for the Dotials, and the words milksops and 'sissies' were freely bandied about in self-accusation, but it is difficult to conceive a process better calculated to promote universal misery than striking water-logged tents and packing up soaking bedding in a deluge of rain.

We lay in our tents all day watching the drips and rivulets, stabbing holes in the floor to keep the lakes at a reasonable level, and blessing our stars that we were the right side of the Bireh Ganga. It was a day for song if ever there was one; on such a day, pent up in a leaking tent, the most mournful hymns have been found to have a very composing effect. But we were singularly deficient in this useful accomplishment and I do not remember a single chorus. Perhaps we were too serious-minded and certainly the ship was heavily freighted with learning. In one tent you could listen to a discussion on geology or, if not a discussion, at any rate a monologue; in another poetry was not only discussed but also written, while in a third medicine would be the theme, for we boasted no less than two doctors in embryo, and one ci-devant. It was possible to have a fellow-feeling for Walpole, the Prime Minister, who said that he always encouraged the guests at his table to talk bawdy because that was a subject in which everyone could join.

So many would-be doctors were rather a thorn in the flesh at times, because there was a ban on unboiled water and it was impossible to drink out of a stream unless they were out of sight, and then it was done furtively and with a sense of guilt. Even some apples which we got in Joshimath, straight off a tree, were subjected to the indignity of a potassium permanganate bath; I suppose they deserved it for not moving with the times, and omitting to grow a cellophane wrapper as well as a skin.

Meantime it is still raining, as it was when this digression started, and so it continued for a second night until by dawn it had rained itself out. After crossing another 11,000 ft. ridge above Kaliaghat we dropped again to the stream which had to be forded. The approach to it was down the loose debris of a comparatively recent landslide, flanked on the right by the horribly unstable-looking precipice of yellow rock off which the slip had broken. The road crosses the river below a waterfall issuing from a gorge which is almost a cave, and which Loomis compared to the Bee Rocks of *The Jungle Book*. Normally this ford is only ankle deep but now it was impracticable, and we had to cross by a fresh place a hundred yards down stream where the bed widened. The previous day even this would have been impassable, as the porters had feared.

On the far side we passed many clumps of bamboo and, partly for old times' sake, and to amuse the others, I got the Sherpas to gather some young shoots, which we had cooked for dinner. On one occasion in 1934 bamboo shoots had been our 'manna'. We enjoyed another gastronomic treat that day when we found wild strawberries almost as large as a cultivated variety.

And talking of gastronomy, we ourselves provided a gastronomic treat for the leeches that were here in considerable numbers. It has always puzzled me what these creatures live on in the normal course of a dull life, and whether blood is a necessity. The banquets provided by human beings must be of rare occurrence in the dense, wet, tropical forests which are their usual habitat. We had met a few in the lower country earlier in the march, but it was curious to find so many here at an altitude of over 9000 ft. Leeches have always been associated in my mind with hot, wet climates, but I suppose no one from the forests of Assam or Burma, where there really are leeches, would admit that we had seen any; half-a-dozen on one's feet in the course of a march would to them appear negligible. We found our footgear, or rather lack of footgear, namely rubbers and no socks, as satisfactory as any for combating these revolting beasts. One generally noticed them at once on shoe or bare leg and could pull them off before they had a good hold, whereas boots, socks, and puttees will not prevent them from getting at the feet; the leech on them is harder to spot, and, once in, it is not discovered until the boots are removed in camp and found to be full of blood and gorged leeches.

Now began a long, steep grind to the 12,400 ft. Kuari Pass, but to-day we were bound only for Dekwani, the grazing alp 1000 ft. below the ridge. When we were here in June the air resounded with the bleating of sheep, and white flocks covered the hillside, but now the place was empty of life except for some choughs and a questing hawk. This camping-ground is just above the tree-line and in consequence rather bleak; instead of pitching their tents the Dotials retired to the woods to sleep—only the Europeans were hardy enough to endure the rigours of the tents.

When we passed this way in 1934 we made a special effort to be on top of the Pass at dawn and virtue was for once rewarded by the unsurpassed panorama of the Garhwal Himalaya, which is seen from here in fair weather. But that was in May, and now in this month of rain and mist not much was to be expected, so we were content to be up there by eight o'clock. There was a lot of cloud to the north but all was not hidden and to the majority of our party, who had not yet seen a Himalayan mountain, the little that remained was a breath-taking revelation. Dunagiri to the north-east claimed preeminence of beauty and of stature, and her perfectly proportioned shape shone dazzlingly white in a frame of massive cloud. Across the Dhauli valley the great bulk of Hathi Parbat stood up like an iceberg from a sea of vapour, while to the north, near Badrinath, the country was bathed in sun and the warm glow of a glacier there was for all the world like pink snow.

For long we looked, trying with camera and cinema to capture some record of the changing scene, and then, having added each a stone to the cairn which guards the Pass, we began the long and easy descent. The grass merged into pine forest and 1000 ft. lower, where two tracks diverged, Pasang Kikuli and I turned west for Joshimath while the bandobast* went on down to Tapoban.

---

* Bandobast—a useful term meaning organising or the organisation itself.

CHAPTER VIII

THE RISHI ONCE MORE

◆

IT WAS JULY 19TH when we reached Joshimath and inquiries for Emmons in the bazaar elicited the information that, arriving two days ago, he had gone up to Badrinath and was expected back that day. Having collected the mail, we repaired to the dak bungalow and half an hour later Pasang Kikuli reported that he could see Emmons and Kitar riding up from Vishnuprayag, the temple at the junction of the Dhauli and Alaknanda rivers, 1500 ft. below Joshimath.

A little later he and Kitar arrived and we swopped news. He had thoroughly enjoyed his journey along the Pilgrim Road, particularly the day spent at Badrinath, where he was very kindly received by the Rawal, and shown the Temple, the hot spring, and the steps leading down to the frigid waters of the Alaknanda, where the pilgrims bathe ceremonially, clinging to a ringbolt.

The next to arrive was a wire from Carter saying that he was leaving Ranikhet that day, so that here were two members of the party who had not allowed the grass to grow, however leisurely may have been the progress of the main body.

Finally, in the evening, ten Mana men arrived with the chest-slapping Kalu. Kalu I had hoped was up the valley at Tapoban collecting food, but here he was with the Mana men and, seemingly, rather the worse for wear.

I soon learnt that, if we were relying on him to find coolie food, we might whistle for it; the month that had elapsed since he left us had apparently been spent at Mana or Badrinath, and from his blear-eyed look very ill-spent. I hurried down to the bazaar to see what could be done, but the man I had dealt with previously was away and all that his underling could promise was one load of atta. Here was a pretty kettle of fish, for it might take two or three days to collect the ten loads we wanted and the prospect of further delay was maddening. Returning to the bungalow I gave the Mana men sufficient rupees, and told them to scrape together all the food they could find in the bazaar. The result was beyond expectation, and two hours later they had got together eight loads of atta and two of rice.

Early next morning two Dotials and Phuta came in from Tapoban as arranged, and I spent the morning again in the bazaar buying odds and ends for them and the Bhotias. The Mana men are Bhotias and the name gives some indication of their origin, for Tibet was known as the land of Bhot.

The Garhwal Bhotias number about five hundred, divided between the villages of Mana and Niti. They themselves claim that they are Hindus who crossed the Himalaya into Tibet many generations ago, and after a long sojourn there, during which presumably they inter-married, they returned to their present home. They are not identical with Tibetans, but they are of a Mongolian type, sturdy, thick-set, with olive complexions sometimes tinged on the cheeks with a ruddy glow. The men wear a long blanket coat of homespun reaching to the knees, over trousers of the same material, which are tight at the ankles, baggy above, and tied at the waist like pyjamas. None of them are fanatical about cleanliness.

The village of Mana is 10,500 ft. above the sea and is set on a boul-der-strewn slope, where the low stone houses of the village seem as natural as the great erratic blocks which litter the hillside. It overlooks the Alaknanda river at its confluence with the Saraswati and only a few miles below the glacier source of the first-named. The shrine at this river junction is called Keshoprayag and is sacred to Vishnu. Imme-diately above here the Saraswati flows through a very remarkable cleft, the walls of which almost touch above, the river flowing heard but unseen several hundred feet below. Some cultivation of barley and buckwheat is carried on and there is one tree, of which the Mana people are rightly proud; but sheep, goats, and the Tibetan trade are their main interest.

The trade from Mana is neither so extensive nor so lucrative as that carried on over the eastern passes from the Milam valley in Almora. The Mana Pass is 18,650 ft. and comparatively more difficult than the others, and the trade seems to have fallen off considerably in recent years. Here, as in Milam, the Tibetan Jongpen sends an official to Mana to ascertain whether there is any disease amongst men or cattle before declaring the Pass open for the summer. The official is given a stone (who determines the size I have not learnt) and the Bhotias undertake to forfeit its weight in gold if any disease be introduced into Tibet. A licence to trade has to be paid for in cash or kind, and a commission is exacted on all deals. The chief exports are food-stuffs of all kinds, cloth, sugar, spices, tobacco, and dried fruits; and the imports salt, borax, wool, ponies, dogs, jubus (a cross between a yak and a cow), rugs, Tibetan saddles, tea, butter, gold, yak tails, and horns.

Now that we were about to leave the habitations of men, our porters had to be supplied with a few extras, both luxuries and necessities, and it was interesting to compare the respective wants of our three different breeds.

The Bhotias' needs were hard to satisfy either in variety or quantity. They evidently believed in doing themselves well if someone else footed the bill, and seemed not to have heard anything about pipers and the tunes they played. Eight pounds of tobacco was their first demand, cut down by me to four; then half-a-dozen different spices were selected and equal quantities of red and black lentils. Ghee was the next item, and several shops were visited before a superfine quality was found, and then I had to put in another demurrer as to quantity, for good ghee is more expensive than butter. Several 2 lb. cakes of jaggery wrapped in leaves were next added to the growing pile; it is unrefined sugar like solidified treacle and indistinguishable from their tobacco. Tea and salt were bought after another wrangle over quantities, for they seemed to think they were fitting out for a year.

That met, if it did not satisfy, their wants, and I wondered apprehensively whether the Dotials had the same generous notions about what was requisite for their well-being. Fortunately the headman himself had not come, no doubt only because he realised that something might have to be carried back, and the two men he had sent had not been properly coached. When asked what they wanted, they were quite at a loss, and tea, sugar, salt, and tobacco had to be pressed on them. The Sherpas' needs were similar to the Bhotias', except that they took cigarettes instead of tobacco, and made no attempt to take advantage of having *carte blanche* to get what they wanted.

While this was going on, Loomis and Lloyd arrived, having come in to see the sights of the metropolis, and at one o'clock we all started

Mana village

Mana porters

back together carrying the morning's purchases, ten loads of coolie food, and some apples for ourselves. There is a small orchard at Joshimath and earlier in the year peaches of enormous size can be had.

Before leaving, arrangements were made for Carter's possible coming, and instead of turning Kalu off, as he deserved, I gave him the job of waiting here to take charge of Carter when he arrived and, with the help of another Mana man, to follow us into the Basin. He was very repentant, praying constantly with his hands palm to palm, and seemed pleased at having this responsibility put upon him.

We reached Tapoban at three o'clock and, jealous of the others who had spent the morning wallowing in the hot bath, we three lost no time in visiting it. To our annoyance the hermit was there sitting outside the hut, his long hair reaching to the ground, and his eyes fixed vacantly on the stone tank. It is *infra dig.* to strip in front of natives, but I got rid of him by the simple expedient of holding out a four-anna piece and pointing to the hut. His mind was not as blank as his face, for he at once understood, got up and went into his hut, and I placed the money on the stone thus vacated. When we had done boiling ourselves and dashing from the hot to the cold and back again, he came out of the hut, took up the money, and resumed his contemplation of the infinite.

The camping-place at Tapoban is on a grass plateau the size of a tennis court, which has the appearance of having once been part of a fort. Close by are three very old and completely neglected shrines, beautifully built of massive stone put together without any mortar. They are said to date back to A.D. 800. The only inhabited building nearby is a school for the children of the neighbouring villages. After school hours it serves the purpose of an inn, for I remember we slept in it in 1934 and now it sheltered the Mana men. Some slight readjustments of loads were made here when most of us found we had brought too much, and some articles of food found to be in excess were also left. From these we made up an assortment of food for Carter's use, and the whole was handed over to the care of the schoolmaster.

It was important that the Dotials and the Mana men should get on well together, but I had always had a lurking fear that this pious hope would not be realised—that in fact it might be far otherwise. The Bhotias did not strike one as being good mixers, although they were friendly enough with the Sherpas, but I think they despised the Dotials and resented the fact that we were employing them instead of Bhotias. I watched them when they first met that evening and, though neither side was effusive, they talked together a little, in a distant manner, like two strange dogs smelling round each other. Once the ice was broken I hoped that good relations would be established, but an incident next morning showed that of this there was little likelihood.

The Mana men were as usual the last to start, and as they were coming up the road to collect their loads they met the Dotials starting off, already laden. Unfortunately one of the Dotials had taken one of the food loads which the Mana men had brought yesterday from Joshi-math—a handy compact bag of 60 lb., very comfortable to carry. The Mana men had marked all their loads and promptly claimed this one. The Dotial refused to give it up and both sides gathered round to join in the argument. We were still at the camp, but the row attracted our attention and I hurried down to see what was happening. All loads had been downed and the more hot-tempered on both sides were shouting and grimacing and threatening each other with fists and sticks. The headman, instead of pacifying them, had got his face about an inch off the head Bhotia's, shouting away with the best. A first-class riot seemed imminent. They were so excited that little attention was paid to me, but with the arrival of one or two Sahibs we managed to separate them, and giving the Mana man his load sent them off out of the way. The Dotial who had been the most aggressive in flourishing his stick I paid off and sacked on the spot, 'pour en-courager les autres', and in the heat of the moment overpaid him to the extent of Rs 7. Perhaps this was lucky, because without that accidental inducement he might have refused to go home alone and would probably have been backed up by his fellows. He was the strongest of the Dotials and a good man, and I was sorry to lose him.

Later, when I caught up with the Mana men, I gave them a talk-ing to, and declared fiercely that at the least sign of trouble they would all be sacked—a piece of bluff which to have had called would have been exceedingly inconvenient. For the next day or two I lived in con-stant dread that some triviality would blow up the smouldering fires, and took care not to leave them alone together on the march. There were no rows but there was no cordiality, and the notion previously entertained, that the Mana men would extend a helping hand to a Dotial in difficulties, was obviously false—they were more likely to push him down the *khud*.

Our route that day followed the Dhauli valley, and the aspect of this valley differed widely from those mild and beautiful valleys which we had crossed on the way to Joshimath. Here the scene was grander and sterner, in places almost savage, and no imagination was required to guess that close behind the steep enclosing walls lay the ice, rock, and snow of high mountains. The Dhauli river rises near the Niti Pass and its course down to Tapoban is almost one great gorge, through the bed of which the water roars and rages with incredible violence. It is milky white with glacial deposits.

Four miles above Tapoban, where the road crossed by a stout cantilever bridge from the south to the north side of the river, the Rishi Ganga flows into the Dhauli. We looked with newly awakened interest at the grey rushing waters that were a living witness to the mysterious Basin, and at the gorge above which still kept its secrets.

Beyond this we recrossed to the south bank of the Dhauli by a rather amateurish suspension bridge, the flimsy flooring sagging and swaying a few feet above the boiling water that dizzied the eye to look upon. Frail though it was, it was comforting to feel that two-foot wide flooring underfoot, unlike the home-made bamboo bridges of Sikkim, where one shuffles one foot after the other along two slippery bamboos, clinging affectionately to the handrail the while.

After crossing the bridge we climbed up from the river to the village of Lata, the porters sweating hard and resting frequently under a hot sun, which we noticed was surrounded by a wide halo. Lata is no place to camp at if it can be avoided, but the next water is a long way up the hill, and the need of shelter and food for the coolies make it advisable to stop near a village if there is one. One very remarkable fact about this village was that there were three eggs in it, but even this paled before the yet more remarkable fact that the owner wanted half a rupee (about 9d.) for each of them.

Lata was the last link with the outside world, and from now on we and our fifty-three porters were dependent for food and shelter on what we carried. We could not afford to waste any days now, for when the porters are not marching they still eat. They were consuming nearly one hundred pounds of food every day and the number of days we could keep them was dictated by the food we had. Of course the longer their services were available the farther, within limits, we could push our base, and any time wasted meant that we should have to dismiss them before this goal was reached.

Bad weather might hold us up, as it had at Kaliaghat, and it was with gloomy foreboding that we observed the sun halo, but the next day turned out as fine as any we had had. The road climbed almost without a break for 5000 ft. to Lata Kharak, which was our camping-ground. It is a grassy hollow just above the tree-line, which here is over 12,000 ft.; birch trees and rhododendrons are the only trees able to grow at this height, the pine having given up the struggle a little lower down. One variety of pine which grew here, the 'chir' or *Pinus longifolia*, is a most useful tree because, being full of resin, it burns like a torch, and a few slivers of it make excellent kindling. Pasang Kikuli generally carried some, and with it a fire could be started under the worst conditions. Rhododendron makes a good fire too, but it is not easy to start.

The Dotials were on their mettle to-day and out to show the Mana men what they could do, with the result that they climbed this 5000 ft. in five hours and were in camp by half-past twelve; the Bhotias took it easy, as they usually did, and were not up until two o'clock. A chill wind and mist are the rule at this camp but to-day it was fine and warm. The Mana men retired to the woods to sleep, despising tents at this moderate altitude even had tents been available, as they were not. The Dotials occupied all there were, probably more with a view to depriving the Mana men of them than from any renewed faith in their weather-resisting powers.

It was wet when we got up at half-past five, but when we started two hours later this had turned to fine mist. The crest of the ridge overlooking the Rishi valley from the north is first gained at a height of about 13,000 ft., and then the path traverses along the north side, ascending gently, until it crosses the ridge by the 14,000 ft. Durashi Pass. From the Pass views of peaks both to north and south should be obtained, but though we sat there an hour to give it a chance, the mist refused to lift. From here a sensational traverse leads across a mile of some of the steepest and most rugged cliffs imaginable. At first glance a man would despair of getting himself across, let alone a flock of sheep, but every summer many hundreds of sheep and goats are taken over it, and back again in the autumn with young lambs at foot. In May, when there is snow and ice about, step-cutting is necessary, but when the snow has gone all is plain sailing and it is merely an airy walk.

At the further end of the traverse is much dead juniper wood, and those who know the scarcity of fuel at Durashi add as much of this as they can carry to their loads. The traverse ends in a long steep gully full of loose stones, and at the bottom of this I waited to see the porters come down, thinking that someone might get hit by a stone. I need not have worried—not even a pebble was dislodged. A steeper but shorter gully was then climbed and there below us lay Durashi, but no tinkle of sheep bells reached our ears, and the place was apparently deserted. The Bhotias accounted for this by saying there was not enough grass, but I think it more likely that the shepherds had been driven out by excessive rain; sheep had certainly been there recently.

We had already reduced the loads appreciably by eating, and now we were able to pay off five Dotials, which made a useful reduction in the number of mouths to be fed. I had expected some trouble in select-ing the five victims, but two of them chose themselves by being sick and the other three made no bones about going. The Dotials are much more amenable than the Bhotias; when Loomis and I were here in June I had tried to send some of the Mana men back because there were no longer any loads for them, but it only led to trouble. They presented a united front and said that all would go on or all would go back, so we had to submit to paying and, what was more important, feeding four unnecessary men.

The march between Durashi and Dibrugheta is short, and again, as in June, we lingered long on the 'Curtain' ridge, expectant of a view, for on a clear day Nanda Devi herself is visible. The mist however was thicker than ever and even the Dibrugheta alp immediately below us was hidden. From the ridge to the alp is a drop of some 3000 ft. down an excessively steep grass slope, and the few who now remained faith-ful to rubber shoes had some very unhappy moments, which were accentuated when it began raining. At the bottom is a stream, and the way out up the opposite bank lies over steep rock clothed with a thin layer of mud, grass, and other vegetation. Here it went hard with the rubber school and the porters with awkward loads, one of whom had to have his load carried up piecemeal. This was an unlucky Dotial carrying a load, part of which consisted of tent poles, the most troublesome and impracticable tent poles that ever were. Each pole weighed 4 lb. and was in two sections, each four feet long; one section telescoped into the other but at the slightest provocation telescoped out again. If carried horizontally they caught on every projection near the path, and if carried vertically they bruised either the man's head or his backside. The seven poles made up half the load and the other half was something just as unwieldy but rather less necessary, a glacier drill. This is a scientific instrument and not, as one might suspect from its presence in a mountaineering party, some device to facilitate glacier travel. Of its subsequent history all that need be said is that like the immortal Duke of York's men it 'was marched right up the hill, and then marched down again'.

Having disentangled ourselves from these perplexities we emerged on to the small plateau of the Dibrugheta alp, an emerald gem in a sombre setting of dark green pines. The flowers which, earlier in the year, make this meadow a Joseph's coat were past their best, only a few white anemones remaining to set off the rich crimson of the potentillas. Of greater interest than these to the materially minded were the wild shallots which mingled with them.

It was raining too hard when we arrived for a due appreciation of our surroundings. As Dr Johnson said, 'the noblest prospect is improved by a good inn in the foreground', and no time was lost by us in thus augmenting the beauty of the scene. The tents were pitched, the loads stacked on top of a flat rock and covered with a tarpaulin, and at last a fire was started under a sheltering canopy of umbrellas. At dark the rain ceased, fresh logs were piled on, and we sat round enjoying the blaze like so many salamanders. Then the moon rose, outlining for us in a silver silhouette the summit of Niti peak and emphasising the black profile of the 'Curtain' which towered above us, while, across the dark cleft of the Rishi, pinnacle upon pinnacle of rock was etched against an indigo sky.

CHAPTER IX

TO THE FOOT OF THE GORGE

———◆———

THE SHEEP TRACK WHICH we had so far followed ends at Dibrugheta
and from here to the foot of the gorge and through it the going
becomes progressively difficult; the first stage from Dibrugheta to
the Cave Camp gave the Dotials a taste of what was in store for them
higher up. It might be said of them as of the crew of a more famous
expedition:

> The danger was past—they had landed at last,
> With their boxes, portmanteaus, and bags:
> Yet at first sight the crew were not pleased with the view,
> Which consisted of chasms and crags.

The march begins in a brutally abrupt manner with a stiff climb of
1000 ft. through grand pine forest. We were off before eight on a fine
morning and an hour later had cleared the pines and were sitting on
the ridge getting a first sight of our objective, Nanda Devi. The lower
part was hidden in cloud, giving an added effect of height. Gazing with
wonder at the great wedge of the summit, supported on the south-west
by a fearfully steep sort of flying buttress, all who were looking at the
mountain for the first time were profoundly impressed. In the immediate foreground ravines and ridges alternated with rock walls and grass
slopes to confuse the eye, until in the distance a great grassy shoulder
screened the whole of the upper gorge.

The porters went well and by eleven o'clock we reached what
Shipton and I had christened 'Rhubarb Gully', a gully with a stream
running down it, full of lush vegetation, including a quantity of wild
rhubarb. The porters like to eat the tops of this when it has gone to
seed, but the stems stewed with sugar are every bit as good as the cultivated variety. We ate them whenever we could.

We continued our march, groping our way through thickets of
rhododendron, balancing along narrow ledges of rock, and stepping

gingerly over the smooth water-worn slabs of the ravines, until we reached the most critical piece of the day. This was a smooth cliff several hundred feet high, liberally provided with holds in the shape of grass and short furze. Although I had been up and down it five times I never was fond of it, disliked it especially coming down, and dreaded it when wet. Luckily to-day the rain was holding off and everyone made a special effort to get there before it started. The Mana men in their bare feet simply romped up, and most of the Dotials seemed equally at home, but the little man carrying the tent poles broke down completely. He could not face it, and even after dumping his load he had to be shepherded all the way up, Emmons and I keeping an eye on him from behind while a Dotial in front held his hand. His load was again brought up piecemeal.

There followed a trying half mile over a chaotic scree of enormous blocks, amongst which we dodged and climbed, coming frequently to an impasse. The Cave Camp, reached at three o'clock, consists of one big cave with a very uneven floor and a through-draught which by means of a vent at the back draws the smoke of a fire right through the cave, thoroughly fumigating the occupants. We appropriated this, the Bhotias found another cave, and the Dotials pitched tents in the most unlikely places. There is ample juniper wood here, rhubarb grows luxuriantly, and the cave is dry, so that altogether it is a refuge not to be despised.

In June we had dumped a bag of atta and a bag of rice here and we were relieved to find the atta was only slightly affected by damp. For food on their return journey we now left some atta for the Dotials and some rice for the Bhotias. The Dotials had asked for nothing but atta and this was their sole food, morning and night, in the form of chapatties; nor could they use rice had they wanted it, because they had no cooking pots except the shallow iron bowl in which chapatties are baked.

So far everything had gone well; true, it had rained most days, but this had neither damaged the loads nor depressed the spirits of the porters. But on Sunday, July 26th, the tide of fortune seemed to be on the turn. It rained heavily in the night and in consequence we made a late start, not getting away until nearly nine o'clock. Our destination was the old Base Camp, hereafter called the Bridge Camp, on the south bank of the Rishi, and to get there we had to go over the big grass shoulder and cross the Rhamani torrent which lay beyond. Neither in 1934 nor in June this year had we experienced much trouble in crossing this stream provided it was tackled before afternoon. It is fed by a glacier and like all such streams it increased in volume as the day wore on, reaching its maximum at evening, owing to the melting of the glacier as the warmth increased. With this in front of us then, it was desirable to make an early start, but having failed to do this I tried to keep the porters moving and was not unduly worried about the river.

We reached the top of the grass shoulder at midday, when the mist which had been hanging about all morning turned to rain. This was fortunate in a way because the ridge was a favourite halting-place for the Mana men, who loved to sit there and smoke. On fine days there is a magnificent view of Nanda Devi and the gorge. We were quickly driven off by rain, which increased in intensity as we descended to the Rhamani until it became so blinding that it was difficult to find the crossing-place. It was essential to hit off the right place because the Rhamani flows in a miniature box canyon and in that place only was it possible to climb out on the other side.

When we finally reached the river at one o'clock it was running fast and high and looked very uninviting. Loomis and I waded out, tentatively, hand-in-hand and tied to a rope. We got about half-way and then turned back, for it was over our thighs, or at any rate mine, and running too fast for the porters to be expected to face it. Various futile expedients were tried, such as pushing big boulders into the water. This was the Sherpas' idea, but I think it was more for the pleasure of seeing a boulder go in than from any thought-out plan. A boulder of anything less than five hundredweight would not stand against the current, but there were plenty of big ones about and the Sherpas managed to roll one of nearly half a ton down the bank into the water and the prodigious splash it made was greeted with happy cries—it was a comfort to know that someone was getting some fun out of our predicament. Operations then ceased, for even they were not capable of standing on this and dropping another of equal weight on the far side of it, and so on until the fifty feet of rushing water were bridged.

We cast up and down the bank, but fifty yards either way was all that could be made before cliffs barred further progress. Meantime we were all very wet and cold and it was at last borne in upon us that we must wait here for better times. The word was given to camp, and soon the already water-logged tents were pitched on the narrow bed of shingle, and the Bhotias, as was their way, had found a snug cave some way above the river. It was the more annoying to be stopped because once across the Rhamani it was no great distance to the Bridge Camp.

Within an hour of our arrival the river appeared to rise another foot but after that it began to drop a little. Our camp was quite safe because we were six or seven feet above the water, but it was puzzling to know whether the rise was caused mainly by rain or was merely due to the melting of the glacier. If the rain had brought it about we might be here for a day or two, for there was no sign of it stopping, but we hoped that most of the rise was normal, in which case we should be able to get over early in the morning.

We found an overhang that gave enough protection to keep a fire going, and after a hot meal we felt more cheerful, though the outlook was gloomy enough. Before dark I had a talk with the Dotials and told them I wanted four more to return from here. The headman approved of that and though he confessed to being sick himself he did not ask to be one of the four. This sudden illness was probably diplomatic, but had he been at death's door he could not have looked a greater picture of woe, squatting under a tattered umbrella with his head enveloped in a pink shawl. On that I went to bed, but the noise of the river, which seemed to have a note of malice in it, made sleep difficult. Just as I was dozing off a head was thrust through the tent door and a torrent of words rose high above the roar of the river. It was one of the Dotials, the most vocal of them, a demagogue with a fearful rush of words to the mouth. By his tone I guessed he had not come to tuck me in and say 'goodnight', but it was some time before I grasped the gist of his tirade—they were all going home.

He had chosen the best time for belling the cat because I was not sufficiently awake to be interested and could only tell him to take his face out of the door and shut both. The news was disturbing but was not taken very seriously, and I thought that tactful handling and a lower river would bring about a change of mind.

It rained all night and was still drizzling at dawn when I went outside to have a look at the river. It was still pretty high, but better than yesterday, and routing out Loomis I got him to hold the rope while I went over. We then hauled the rope taut and made fast at each end, spanning the stream, and I hoped that this little surprise, arranged for their benefit, would put fresh heart into the Dotials. Early morning bathing in glacier streams might be enjoyed by the hardy souls who break the ice in the Serpentine, but for my part I made a beeline for the kitchen fire to still my chattering teeth.

Here Nima pointed with glee to a great slab of rock which had peeled off the rock of the overhang in the night, falling flat on the fire-place. Another piece now threatened to do the same, but Nima was blowing away at the fire quite indifferently. A Sherpa blowing up a fire is a rare spectacle. He has only to put his head down, and after a few well-directed and long-drawn blasts, which scatter wood and ashes in all directions, a fire which is seemingly past praying for will burst crack-ling into life; and for dealing with fires, and all that fires imply, food, drink, and warmth, which in this sort of life seem almost as important as life itself, they possess equally useful adjuncts in hands which can lift up live coals and boiling saucepans, and in eyes and lungs which are impervious to smoke.

The Dotials were now stirring, but when they saw the rope across the river it was not greeted with the joyous and enthusiastic shouts that we expected, and presently my eloquent friend of last night was reaffirming their determination to have nothing to do with the river. I told him the river was lower, there was a rope to hang on to, and that all the loads would be put across for them, and on that he retired to take the sense of the meeting. After breakfast the Bhotias descended from their cave and their resourceful minds soon hit on the right method for roping the loads over, putting our scientific brains to shame. Several of them went across by the fixed rope and took up a position on a rock ten feet above the water; others took up a position high up on a cliff on our side immediately opposite. Two 120 ft. climb-ing ropes were slung across and soon the loads were being tied on and hauled over as fast as they could be carried up the cliff. The fact that the taking-off place was much higher than the landing-place made the hauling quite light work.

The Dotials helped us in getting the loads up instead of sulking as might have been expected, and from this I argued they were going

Mana men crossing Rhamani by fixed rope

to change their minds and come with us. No loads fell in, the last went over, and then the remaining Bhotias and Sherpas crossed followed by the Sahibs.

It was beginning to rain again when I turned to make a last fervent appeal to the Dotials before crossing myself. The headman, still under his umbrella and wrapped closer than ever in his pink shawl, looked yet more disconsolate and took no interest in the proceedings. I asked for a few to cross, even if only to carry our loads to the Bridge Camp, but the only response to all entreaties was that they were frightened of the river, and that they wanted to be paid off and dismissed. It was time to play the last card, a card that I fondly hoped would be a trump, and I pointed out that all the money was now on the other side so that they would have to cross anyhow to get their pay—to which the reply was, that I could go across and fetch it back.

For a moment it looked as if they would go home without their pay, but bribing one of them with the gift of my umbrella, I persuaded him to cross with me hand-in-hand. The rupees were unpacked and, sitting by the river, with Pasang holding the umbrella over us, we counted out the money due. The transaction was soon completed, for the envoy was too cold and wet to argue about it, and we were spared the importunities of the whole mob for more baksheesh, and the abuse of the headman at receiving none. The man recrossed and with no more ado the Dotials climbed out of the river bed and disappeared in the driving rain.

We discovered much later, on the way back in fact, that they took it out of the Mana men by eating or taking away all the rice left at the Cave Camp, which was two days' rations for the Mana men, a mean act which might have had serious consequences for anyone less tough and less able to look after themselves than the Bhotias.

It was time to consider our own position. Our porter strength was now sixteen instead of forty-eight, but by increasing the Sahibs' loads to 60 lb. we could reckon on shifting about twenty full loads. We still hoped to reach the Bridge Camp that day, and if everyone piled on a bit extra all the loads might be got there in two journeys. The route followed the precipitous bank of the Rhamani down to its junction with the Rishi, a distance of about half a mile. Just above the junction was the natural bridge across the Rishi formed by a giant boulder, but

Foot of Gorge, Bridge Camp, *circa* 11,500 ft.

the short approach to the bridge was a sheer wall and loads had to be lowered down. The rock of the bridge too was smooth and slippery, as was the descent on the far side, but all these places had been made easy, if not very safe, when we were here in June by fixing branches as ladders. The camp was only a couple of hundred yards upstream from the crossing-place.

The Bhotias seemed in good heart, rather pleased, I imagined, at the defection of the Dotials, and carrying very big loads we cautiously began the descent to the Rishi. It was infernally steep and slippery, but we got down to a point close above the bridge without incident, dumped the loads there under a tarpaulin, and went back for the remainder. It seemed to me that if we went right on to the camp with this lot it would, under the prevailing weather conditions, be difficult to make anyone turn out again.

By midday everything was assembled at the dump. The loads had then to be carried down to the roping-up place and Loomis and I went down first to receive them as they were lowered. The first load to come down however was received, not by us, but by the Rishi. Apparently Phuta slipped while approaching the dump, which was about 100 ft. higher up; he managed to stop himself rolling, but his load shot down the slope, just missed the party who were busy tying loads on, flew past Loomis' head, and on into the river. I was still lower down and just caught sight of a two-gallon tin of paraffin and the fragments of an oxygen cylinder spinning through the air before they hit the water. I was not sorry to see the oxygen thus taken off our hands, for clearly the time had come for some more scrapping, but the loss of the paraffin could be ill afforded. [The oxygen apparatus had not been brought to assist climbers, but for use in case of illness or frost-bite.]

After this Phuta, very shaken and frightened, was lowered down and parked out of harm's way near the bridge. Then the loads began to arrive, not unaccompanied by small stones, and soon there were enough assembled for the Mana men to start carrying them across the bridge. It was desperately cold work standing there in the pitiless rain and the first fine enthusiasm of the men was evidently on the wane. Once they had carried a load over and dumped it under a convenient overhang it became increasingly difficult to make them leave the shelter for another journey.

At long last everything was down and all hands turned to carrying across the bridge. Bridge is not quite the word for a place where
you first had to climb down a wet slab putting all your weight on a
branch of wood—a branch for the apparent security of which no one
could see any valid physical reason—then to step across a narrow gap
with the river roaring and boiling twenty feet below, traverse across
another slab and finally descend to terra firma by another branch.
But by now the Mana men had had enough and began drifting away
to a cave which one of them had discovered on the Rhamani side,
and in which he had started a fire. The Sherpas were still good for
a bit, and with them we started carrying loads up the south bank of
the Rishi to the camp site, which was quite close. It consists of a big
overhang which is usually bone-dry but where now there was hardly a
dry spot. At four o'clock we called it a day; there were still a number
of loads by the bridge, but we had enough for our immediate needs
and the call of hot tea and food was too insistent.

The chronic state of wetness of our clothes, sleeping bags, and
tents did not make for cheerfulness as we discussed the turn which
events had taken. For the moment our star was not in the ascendant,
but the situation was by no means bad. By cutting down weight a
little, only one relay would be necessary and no load need be more
than 60 lb.; nor had I any fear of the Bhotias leaving us in the lurch,
for they had worked like Trojans until cold and wet finished them.
Indeed in one respect the loss of the Dotials could be borne phil-
osophically, if not cheerfully, in that I felt our responsibilities were
considerably lightened, and there was now no doubt of our having
sufficient food for the porters. I still think it was the river which upset
the Dotials and that in good weather we could have got them up the
worst part of the gorge, now immediately ahead of us, though some of
them might have needed a lot of assistance.

Against these meagre benefits was the fact that it was going to
take us longer to reach the mountain and that there would be less
time available for climbing it, and, moreover, that from now onwards
we ourselves would have to carry heavy loads—not the best prepara-
tion, I thought, for heavy climbing. If we did, it would be 'magnificent but not war', that is we would be exhausting ourselves before
ever the mountain was reached. In most Himalayan expeditions the

object is to spare the climbers any work at all until on the mountain in order to conserve their strength, and here were we proposing to carry 50 or 60 lb. loads over difficult country for the next ten days or more. The alternative of carrying nothing ourselves and leaving it all to the Sherpas and Mana men meant that the extra time required would not leave us enough food to finish the job. These preconceived ideas were upset and our policy justified by the event.

For all that, I felt that my misplaced confidence in the Dotials had let the party in for this and would not have been surprised to hear some hard things said. But there was not a word of reproach and the aim of all seemed now, more than ever, to be to spend themselves rather than spare.

CHAPTER X

THE GORGE

◆───────

T HE DAY AFTER THESE MEMORABLE EVENTS dawned fine, and having discussed the position and decided on a plan, we started sorting out loads and rebagging the food. Food was almost the only item on which much weight could be saved, so it was arranged that only enough for forty days should be taken on from here. Having fixed the amount of each kind, it was easy to fill in the varieties, for by now we knew our likes and dislikes. Even so it was a long job which was only just finished before the rain began again at ten o'clock.

One other way in which weight was saved was the abandonment of two pressure cookers. Their scrapping did cause us some heart-burning, since it was from here onwards that their need would be felt. Cooking at high altitudes becomes difficult owing to the low temperature at which water boils; even at 15,000 ft. this temperature is 85 degrees instead of 100 degrees and of course it decreases as you go higher. Tough things like rice, lentils, beans, or dried vegetables will not cook properly at these temperatures, but the difficulty is got over by using a cooker that cooks by steam under pressure, and in which, I think, even a pair of boots would be made edible. It is a thing like a heavy saucepan with a steam-tight lid, fitted with a safety valve, and a whistle which can be adjusted to go off when the desired pressure is reached. We had two of them, and they were left behind with less reluctance because, so far, we had used hardly any rice or lentils—perhaps Loomis and I had had a surfeit of them on the earlier trip.

By the time this work was finished the Mana men had brought everything up from the bridge, and although they were rather expecting to have the day off we persuaded them to make the trip. The plan was to carry some loads as far as the foot of the 'Slabs' and to return here for the night, and at midday we all moved off in drizzling rain carrying 60 lb. loads. It was about 1500 ft. up to the 'Slabs' and the first few hundred feet immediately above camp were as steep and exposed as any part of the route. Numerous birch trees growing out of the cliff face were of great assistance, and provided the branch did not break or the tree pull out bodily it was impossible to fall.

At the top of this bad stretch was a short rock pitch known to us as the 'Birch Tree Wall', where considerable amusement could be had watching the efforts of the purists to climb it with a load on and without a pull from above. The difference of climbing without or with a load is not always realised; when bowed down under a load places, which otherwise would not be given a thought, appear to bristle with difficulties and have to be treated with the utmost respect. The centre of gravity has shifted so much that balance has to be learnt afresh and any slight movement of the load may have very untoward results. The Bhotias carry their loads by shoulder straps as we do, but the Sherpas and the Dotials use a head strap which must be far more unsafe for any delicate climbing. On this trip we had brought light carrying frames provided with a belly band which did much to obviate the risk of a load shifting. They were very successful, but, without careful adjustment and judicious padding, at the end of a long day one's back felt as though it had been flagellated.

For the remaining thousand feet there was little difficulty but much labour, and it was with sighs of relief that we dragged ourselves up to the cairn, built in 1934, which marks the end of the climb. From here we descended slightly to a wide grass ledge lying at the foot of a rock wall, and a short way along this we dumped the loads under a little overhang. Taking a couple of Mana men, a quantity of light line, and some rock pitons, I went on up the shallow rock chimney leading to the top of the wall and the foot of the 'Slabs'. We secured the rope at the top of these by means of the pitons so that it hung down the full length of the 'Slabs', affording invaluable assistance to a laden man. This done, we started back and reached the Bridge Camp in an hour, thoroughly wet, but very pleased with our day's work.

Next morning, the 29th, was again fine, and we took advantage of it to do some much-needed drying before packing up. The 'Slabs' were reached by ten-thirty and the slow business of getting the loads up began. Some were busy carrying up the 'Slabs' from the dump while others attended to hauling them up the wall. Luckily the rocks were

Halfway Camp (13,000 ft.)

dry, everyone worked with a will, and by one o'clock all were got up without incident.

From here it took nearly two hours to cover the mile to Halfway Camp with half the loads; the route is intricate, involving much up and down work, and there are one or two bad places. The height of this camp is about 13,000 ft. and it is sited on a very uneven boulder-strewn ridge on which the making of tent platforms is hard work.

It was almost three o'clock when we reached it, and it would have been pleasant to devote the rest of the day to making ourselves comfortable. The Sherpas and the Mana men were of this opinion and lost no time in getting to work digging out boulders and levelling sites. It seemed a pity to disturb them, but I had to remind them that the remainder of the loads had still to be brought from the 'Slabs'. It took some time to overcome their passive resistance to this suggestion but finally all, less Graham Brown and Emmons, started back for a second load.

When put to it the Mana men can move at tremendous speed over rough country, and on this occasion we were left toiling hopelessly in the rear. Knowing their leisurely way, one could only surmise that they had gone mad, but there was method in this madness because the first on the scene had the pick of the loads. There was not much to choose as far as weight went, but we still had our old friends the tent poles with us, and there were other loads which vied with them in popularity, such as a sack of miscellaneous junk of which the least angular part was the needle-pointed tripod legs of a plane table; and there were several sacks of sugar which had got wet and started to sweat, so that the shirt of anyone unlucky enough to carry one became like a treacle paper for catching moths.

Better time was made on this second journey, camp being reached soon after five. Graham Brown and Emmons had delved out a tent platform and it was not long before the Sherpas had us all comfortably housed. I say the Sherpas, because at work such as this they are in a class by themselves. No boulder is too big for them and no trouble too great, and when they set to work on a tent platform they remind me of so many terriers digging away at a rat hole.

We were blessed with another fine morning, so that it seemed as though fortune had relented and was smiling on us again. Whilst we

Cliffs in the Gorge

The 'mauvais pas'

were tackling these two difficult stages of the gorge, one of which was now completed, dry weather was an inestimable boon. Of the two I think that over the upper half of the gorge is the worse. There is no place so awkward that loads have to be taken off and roped up, but there are many which are very exposed, which cannot be made safe, and where a slip would be fatal.

To-day we reversed the procedure, taking the camp forward and leaving the rest of the loads to be fetched next day. A gully of smooth water-worn slabs had first to be crossed, where the rubber-footwear school could for once tread with more confidence than those clad in orthodox nailed boots. A gently descending terrace brought us to the crux of this part of the route, a place which in 1934 had earned the name of the 'mauvais pas', and for which, at least on my part, famil-iarity had bred no contempt. Here the general angle steepens until, when standing, you can touch the slope with your elbow. A narrow grass ledge leads to a projecting nose of rock which has to be rounded and then, with no pause, a short steep chimney leads down to another narrow ledge. This continues for about fifty yards of varying degrees of difficulty until finally a high rock bulge is surmounted and the security of a wide terrace reached. The whole distance is so great that there is no means of securing anyone engaged on this traverse, nor is any encour-agement derived from the prospect below, where the steep rock and grass slope continues relentlessly to the river a thousand feet below.

The Mana men crossed unperturbed and did not even bother to wait for us at the other end. I took off my shoes and made the Sher-pas take off theirs—an advisable precaution, because the trouble with these sort of places was that as more people went over them so they got worse. Many of the footholds were grass tufts and by the time the last man used them they were reduced to a small sloping rugosity of slippery earth. One or two of the Sherpas were unable to negotiate the rock nose and Pasang enjoyed himself carrying their loads for them; he was always ready with a helping hand for the weaker. We made three journeys over the 'mauvais pas' and on each were lucky enough to have it dry; when wet it is hazardous, and once in 1934 when there was a covering of fresh snow it became a nightmare.

Descending by easy grass terraces the route approached the river and the Pisgah Buttress, the last defence of the gorge, and so called because from it can be seen the Promised Land of the Sanctuary. It is a great buttress of rock which springs sheer from the river and then slants less steeply upwards for 2000 ft. The original route in 1934 dropped almost to the river before turning to ascend the gully and grass spur flanking the buttress; but the Mana men have improved on this, and now, by what we called the 'Mana variation', the old route is joined high up the grass spur so that descent to the river is avoided.

This 'variation' we took, and though in places rather exposed it saved us a lot of hard work. From where the routes joined we climbed a slope almost bare of grass. Working over to the left, we gained a grass terrace backed by a high wall, up which we climbed by means of a rock staircase. On top were slabs, overlapping like tiles on a roof, but set at a moderate angle, and these took us up to another grass terrace, where we rested before tackling the final problem. This was a vertical rock wall only about ten feet high, and a little overhanging chimney was the solution. With a load on, it was a severe struggle, but there were plenty of willing hands above and below. From here to the ridge of Pisgah was long and steep, and Nuri's condition began to cause us some anxiety. He was going slower and slower and at last gave out altogether, so we relieved him of his load and told him to come on at his own pace.

It was nearing two o'clock as we approached the crest of the ridge, but the sun still shone in a clear sky and as we finished the climb and stepped round a rock boss out onto the ridge, Nanda Devi stood there in all her majesty, the cloud veil for once rent aside. All eyes were drawn to the south ridge on which our hopes centred and we prayed that the face which it hid might be less grim than the profile.

Camp was but a short distance away and we took up our quarters on a ledge in front of the low cave in which Loomis and the Bhotias had dumped the seven bags of food in June. It would not hold a tent and sites for these had to be made, a task that the Sherpas set about in their indefatigable manner, digging out and heaving down phenomenal lumps of rock which in their descent threatened to demolish the Mana men who were camped below.

Some of the food bags that had been left here were found to be damp; we turned them all out, spread the flour and satu in the sun, and rebagged it in dry bags. Only about five pounds from each bag had to be thrown away.

Nuri had to be helped into camp and our united medical talent did their best to diagnose his case without much success.

The days spent at Pisgah camp we shall not easily forget. Apart from the view of Nanda Devi, which is probably more striking from here than from anywhere else, a good part of the northern Basin lies spread out below one like a coloured map. In the middle is the great main glacier which terminates in a hundred feet ice wall from beneath which the Rishi rushes; on the left are smooth grass downs broken only by the white moraine of the Changabang glacier; on the right are the variegated rocks, rust red, yellow, and black, of Nanda Devi's pedestal, while in the far background the kindly grass runs up to warm-coloured scree, the scree merges into glacier, and high over all towers the crenulated snow wall of the Basin.

During the two days spent here we were privileged to see all this not only under a bright sun and blue sky but also by the light of a full moon. Even when we had done admiring the miracle of colour performed at sunset, the distant snow-white wall would be suffused with the delicate pink flush of the afterglow; and then as this faded, snow blending with greying sky as the stage was darkened, the curtain rose gradually on yet a third scene. The grey of the sky changed to steely blue, and the snow wall, at first vaguely outlined, shone out clearly like white marble as the moon sailed up from behind a screen of jet-black rock.

The last day of July dawned fine and after a more leisurely breakfast than usual we started back for Halfway Camp. Nuri, who was a very sick man, and three Sahibs remained behind, as there were only nineteen loads to be fetched. The Mana men again set a furious pace and as we were descending the 'variation' we could see them on the 'mauvais pas'. Going flat out, we did the journey in an hour and they must have beaten us by nearly fifteen minutes. It would be interesting to enter some of those men for the Guides' Race at Grasmere where, I feel sure, they would astonish the natives.

Travelling unladen after a week of heavy packing, one felt as if walking on a different planet, perhaps Mars, where the force of gravity is but half that of the earth. Even so the 'mauvais pas' was treated with respect, and on the return journey, grievously burdened as we were, with much more.

Looking down the Gorge from below Pisgah

We were back soon after one o'clock, observing on the way the beautiful sky phenomenon of an iridescent cloud. The border of a high patch of cirrus cloud appears coloured like a rainbow, the red and green being particularly clear. Until recently their origin was not known, but it is now believed that these coloured patches are fragments of unusually large and brilliant coronae, a corona consisting of a number of concentric rings, rainbow-coloured, which are sometimes seen round the sun or moon when it is covered by a thin cloud veil. It is caused by refracted light from the ice particles which form high cirrus cloud and differs from a halo in having a much smaller radius and a reverse order of colours, blue near the sun and red farthest away. Coronae can be seen frequently round the moon and no doubt they form often round the sun, but owing to the intensity of the light they can only be observed under favourable conditions. I have seen both iridescent cloud and sun halos several times in the Himalaya but nowhere else. They are common in northern regions.

A sun halo is usually regarded as heralding the approach of bad weather, but the period between the omen and the event is indefinite. It seemed to be hardly ever less than a day, but sometimes there was no change in the weather for several days; indeed it was often difficult to see any connection at all between halos and weather. If a corona round the moon is observed and the diameter contracts, it shows that the water particles are uniting into larger ones which may fall in rain; conversely, an expanding corona indicates increasing dryness. The open side of a halo is believed by some to foretell the quarter from which bad weather may be expected. Like most weather signs, halos and coronae are not infallible.

However, the rain, which had held off for so long at this critical time, and now could no longer hinder us, started again the same afternoon. It was with relief and thankfulness that we saw the last load brought into camp and realised that the gorge was now behind us and the way to the mountain lay open.

CHAPTER XI

THE SANCTUARY

I N 1934 THE NEXT CAMP from here was close to the snout of the South
glacier, but it seemed improbable we should be able to get as far as
that with the first loads because we had to return to Pisgah the same
day. However, I had a lingering hope that we might, and accordingly
made a fairly early start.

Most of the precious time thus gained was wasted before we had
gone fifty yards. Close to camp was a broad band of smooth slabs set
at an angle of about 30 degrees, caused by the slipping away of the
surface soil and the exposure of the underlying rock. The Mana men
waltzed across this with no more ado than crossing a road, indeed it
was not unlike crossing a road but, of course, less dangerous, and then
they sat down on the far side to see how we, the eminent mountaineers,
would fare. It was not a prepossessing place to look at and the first few
tentative steps soon convinced us that this time appearances had not
deceived us. The wretched loads were of course the trouble, for with
those on one had not the confidence to stand up boldly and plank the
feet down. Each man took the line that seemed good to him, but all
got into difficulties, and then was seen the comic sight of seven Sahibs
strung out over the slabs in varying attitudes, all betraying uneasiness,
and quite unable to advance. The Mana men, having savoured the
spectacle to the full and allowed time for the indignity of our situation
to sink in, came laughing across the slabs to our aid and led us gently
over by the hand like so many children.

Fighting a way down through a heavy growth of bush, we crossed
a stream, contoured the other side of a valley, and rounding a high
ridge set our faces towards the south. We were now fairly within the
Sanctuary, but there was another hour of very rough going over scree
and boulders before we trod the grass downs for which we were all
longing. After so many days traversing a country so hopelessly askew
as that of the Rishi valley, our ankles had developed a permanent flex,

and great was now the relief and joy of getting them straight again, of walking without having to hold on, and without watching the placing of every step.

Keen as we were to reach the old camp near the glacier, it was difficult if not useless to drive the Bhotias. All that could be done was to push on as fast and as far as possible, and hope that, in their own good time, they would follow; but it was exasperating to look expectantly back and see them sitting like so many crows on some distant ridge over a mile back. At last about two o'clock, when still some one and a half miles from the glacier, I felt that they would not follow much longer, and sat down to wait for them.

A cold wind blew up the valley, but there was a sheltered grass hollow close by a stream which would make a delightful camp. There was no juniper wood at hand, but we had passed some half a mile back and I knew there was more in front. When the Mana men came, an effort was made to get them to push on a little but they assured me there was no water for a long way. Two of them had been here in 1934, and when it came to pitting their memory for a country against mine I was quite prepared to give them best; but later we found that his particular piece of information, which I was not prepared to dispute, was a flat untruth. However, it had been a long march, so we dumped the loads and hurried back, reaching Pisgah about five o'clock. Nuri had been left in camp but appeared no better for the rest, and we wondered how he would manage to-morrow when camp had to be moved. It had been yet another fine day despite the omens of the sky, and again from our vantage point we watched the pageant of setting sun and rising moon, beyond the means of a painter, either in words or colour.

We had carried extra-heavy loads on the first journey, hoping that on the second there would be little left but our personal kit, but when the porters had made up their loads it was so arranged that we had each a tent to shoulder: Nuri was able to travel but of course without a load.

All felt slack, the result of our efforts yesterday. Emmons had gone off at the first streak of light to set up his plane table, but when we joined him at his station halfway to camp he told us he had not been able to fix his position. I was not surprised, because from inside the

The avalanche cone on the way to
Moraine Camp

Crossing the meadows of the Sanctuary,
circa 14,000 ft.

Basin this is by no means easy. To effect it you have to be in a position to see and recognise three known triangulated peaks, all at the same time; and owing to cloud and mist you may have to wait many hours on some bleak and wind-swept spot before this happy event occurs, and when it does you probably mistake one of the peaks and get a completely false result. Before going out to Garhwal in 1934, we had some instruction in plane-table work in Richmond Park, but somehow conditions in the Basin seemed quite different.

Loomis and I reached camp long ahead of the others and impatiently raided the dump for cheese and biscuits, which were still our daily lunch and of which we never tired. On their arrival no time was lost in getting up the tents, for the same cold wind was blowing and presently a drizzling rain set in. The height of this camp was about 14,000 ft. and now for the first time the Mana men condescended to sleep in the despised tents. I confess to some disappointment at this evident sign of degeneration. In 1934, in much the same spot, they appeared quite happy in the lee of a large boulder. Did they but know what our tents were like, their hardihood in proposing to sleep in them might have been admired, but since they expected to find shelter in them their softness was to be lamented. Were the Mana men becoming 'sissies' like their employers?

This camp site was a delicious change after the cramped asperity of the quarters to which we had now been long accustomed, and it was difficult to say which gave us most pleasure, the space, the flatness, or the absence of rock. Below our little hollow the rounded slope curved gently down to the southern branch of the Rishi and the contrast between the opposite bank and our own was as great as it might well be, and could be adequately summed up in the words 'frowning cliffs' and 'smiling downs'. On our side wide slopes of short, sweet grass extended in all directions; a herd of cattle grazing on some distant rise or a flock of sheep coming over the hill would have caused no surprise, so peaceful was the scene. But across the river, savage, reddish-brown cliffs, seamed with dry gullies, rose sheer from the river, presenting a seemingly unbroken alternation of buttress and gully along four straight miles of river frontage; and beyond these the snow and rock of the western ridge of Nanda Devi loomed vaguely in the swirling mists.

It was now August 2nd, and we still had food to feed the Mana men for another five days. Within that time we had to establish a base camp as high up the mountain as we could. The South glacier consists of two main branches which join almost at the snout, one coming in from the south and the other, with which we are concerned, from the south-east. In 1934 we went up this South-East glacier by the true left bank, that is, the side farthest from the mountain, and some two miles up we had found a very pleasant camp at about 16,000 ft.—a sheltered grass flat tucked away behind the moraine and watered by a spring. From this camp we had crossed the glacier, there half a mile wide, and by means of a scree slope gained a serrated rock ridge which, higher up, curled round and merged into the south ridge of Nanda Devi.

It was on this serrated ridge at a height of about 18,000 ft. that we hoped to find a site for a base camp, but the immediate problem was whether to make for the old camp on the far side of the glacier or to go up the unknown right bank. The grassy flat and the spring were very great attractions, but it was more than doubtful if they could be reached in a day from our present camp, so far below the glacier snout. On the other hand by hugging the mountain on the right bank the way would be shortened, and only one camp would be necessary between Sanctuary Camp, where we now were, and the proposed base camp. We decided to eschew the delights of the 1934 camp and to take our chance on the unknown right bank, time being a more important factor than soft lying and spring water.

We got off at eight on the 3rd, all, including Nuri, carrying loads, most of them 60 lb. We had not gone half a mile before coming to a delightful stream of clear water, flanked by an acre patch of dry juni- per wood, the sort of camp one only finds in dreams. I was rather ashamed at not having remembered it myself, but I had no doubt that the Mana men knew of it and could not refrain from asking them how they reconciled this with their statement of two days ago, and whether perhaps the stream and the juniper had both come into existence within the last two years. They had lied, and knew that they had lied, but they were not the least abashed, and laughingly replied that we had gone quite far enough that day and they were not to be blamed, indeed we ought to be grateful to them for furnishing such a good excuse for stopping.

About an hour from camp we came to another of our 1934 camp sites, the one near the snout of the glacier. Cached under a rock were a bag of satu and a spring balance. I opened up the satu and, finding that beneath a hard core the inside was still good, was cautious enough to dry it, rebag it, and add it to our reserve.

Opposite this camp is a tremendous avalanche cone of snow which has slid down one of the gullies of the opposing cliffs and formed a permanent bridge over the Rishi. When it first fell it must have dammed the river, but now this flows underneath it by a passage which it has burrowed out for itself. We crossed by this and climbed up the hard snow of the avalanche for a couple of hundred feet before leaving it for the grass of an old moraine. This took us close under the cliffs at the base of the mountain to a corner where their general direction changed from south to south-east. Here the moraine petered out and we had to commit ourselves to the hummocky, boulder-strewn surface of the South-East glacier. Still hugging the cliffs, we advanced slowly, either on the glacier or in the trough lying between it and the cliffs; on these a wary eye had to be kept, for at one point there was a continuous fall of stones that necessitated a wide detour.

At about midday we halted on top of one of the miniature ice-mountains of the glacier to take stock of our position and to allow the Mana men to catch up, for they were finding it heavy going in bare feet on the rough surface of the glacier, though it was seldom that they had to tread on ice. We eagerly scanned the ground ahead, between the glacier and the base of the mountain, for some suggestion of a camp site, but it was clear that grass flats and springs formed no part of the landscape on this side. Half a mile up was a high bank of talus which looked as though it might conceal something, so, leaving the others, Graham Brown and I pushed on to investigate. When opposite the bank we dumped our loads, got off the glacier, and climbed on to the top of the bank by a stone gully. Following up along the edge we came first to a stream and then to a dry flat of sand and mud lying between moraine and cliffs. It appeared to be clear of stone-falls, so we decided it would do and hastened back to call up the others. Pasang dashed ahead, and before Graham Brown and I had reached the foot of the stone gully he was coming down from the glacier carrying both our loads and his own!

By two o'clock everybody was in and, after a long rest, we started back, satisfied at having found in this wilderness of rock and ice such a comparative oasis, but fearing that it might yet prove too far from where we hoped to put our base camp. While we rested here a herd of bharal, or wild sheep, was seen traversing at a gallop the yellow cliffs nearly 1000 ft. above us and stopping occasionally to utter a sort of shrill whistle. On the grass downs of the Sanctuary there are at least two large herds, but this time we did not come across them. Had we seen any, the sight of so much fresh meat walking about might have made us regret our decision against bringing rifles, but to disturb a peace, which for them has never been broken, would be almost sacrilege, nor were a rifle and ammunition worth their weight for the sake of supplementing an ample diet with an occasional haunch of venison. Shooting for the pot may in some circumstances be necessary, but in the Sanctuary both sentiment and expediency are strongly opposed to it. It has been proposed that the Government of the United Provinces make this a sanctuary in fact as well as in name, and it is to be hoped that the game here will continue to enjoy by law the immunity hitherto conferred on them by reputed inaccessibility.

At this Moraine Camp, as it was subsequently known, there was of course no fuel. The limit of height for the invaluable juniper bush is about 14,000 ft. and the height of this camp was 15,000 ft. It was essential to keep our small stock of paraffin, now reduced to 6 gallons, for use on the mountain, so arrangements had to be made to bring wood up to here and on to the next camp, which we hoped would be our base. I wanted to stock the base camp with fuel for three weeks and use no paraffin at all there.

On August 4th we were able to make a start by bringing up two full loads of wood and the rest of us made what small additions of fuel we could to the loads which had still to be carried from Sanctuary Camp. As soon as we reached the new camp at one o'clock it began to rain heavily and a recess under the cliffs had to be burrowed out in order to light the fire. As far as space and flatness went, it was almost as good as the last camp; with all seven tents pitched, and a neat pile of loads under their tarpaulin, it had a most business-like appearance. In fact some were so attracted by it that there was a suggestion that it should be made our base.

It was I think this proposal—no more than a proposal—that led to a very happy evening and, as we realised later, a very timely one. Loomis, apparently, had been carrying, buried in the recesses of his kit, a small flask of Apricot Brandy, and, on the grounds that we had now reached what could, might, or ought to be our base camp, he was moved to produce it.

The secret had been well kept and when, supper over, our mugs, contrary to custom, were returned to us clean, we assumed that someone was going to make a brew of cocoa. Judge then of our surprise and pleasure when instead of that flaccid beverage this small bottle of beautiful amber liquid appeared, and was with due reverence uncorked. One's sense of smell gets a bit blunted in the course of an expedition—it has to—but grateful, oh most grateful, was the aroma of that Hungarian nectar which by some subtle alchemy overcame the fetid atmosphere of the tent. The flask was small and our pint mugs, seven in all, were large, but Napoleon brandy itself could not have been sipped with such gusto or lingered over so lovingly.

As the brandy was good so it was potent, and that distant country Alaska, of which we had already heard more than a little, assumed, along with its travellers, new and terrifying aspects. The already long glaciers of that frozen land increased in length, the trees which seemingly burgeon on these glaciers grew branches of ice, the thermometer dropped to depths unrecorded by science, the grizzlies were as large as elephants and many times as dangerous, and the mosquitoes were not a whit behind the grizzlies in size or fierceness, but of course many times more numerous. And amid all these manifold horrors our intrepid travellers climbed mountains, living the while on toasted marshmallows and desiccated eggs, inhabiting tents similar to ours, and packing loads which to think of made our backs ache. To echo and amend Dr Johnson, 'Claret for boys, port for men, but Apricot Brandy for heroes.'

CHAPTER XII

THE BASE CAMP

———◆———

THE MORNING FOLLOWING THIS DEBAUCH we sent all the Mana men down the valley for fuel. The Sherpas and ourselves set out with the intention of finding a base camp, carrying 60 lb. and 40 lb. respectively: as the height increased we should find this quite enough, for we hoped to get somewhere near 18,000 ft., which would be higher than most of us had ever been.

We pursued the same tactics as yesterday, keeping where possible in the trough between the glacier and the cliffs, sometimes being forced out on to the glacier. Progress was rather laborious, but in an hour and a half we reached the foot of the scree slope up which Shipton and I had gone in 1934, and this was now the scene of a regrettable incident, nothing less than the loss of one of our scientists. On the way up the glacier Odell, either through excess of zeal or insufficiency of load, had led the field at a rare pace and the field had got rather strung out. By the time we plodders had reached the foot of the scree he was out of sight. I had told him that we had to turn up a scree slope but, perhaps in the traditional absence of mind of the professor, or, more likely, because his eyes were glued to the ground after the manner of geologists and prospectors, he had steamed past without noticing it. We sat there for some time wasting valuable breath, which we should presently need, shouting for him, but with no effect.

I forget what load he was carrying. It may have been, and poetic justice demanded that it should have been, the unmentionable glacier drill; but I hardly think it was, because I remember we were flattering ourselves that that would be dumped at Moraine Camp where there was what seemed to be, at least to our ignorant minds, a fair sample of Himalayan glacier within a stone's throw, waiting to be drilled.

Anyhow we wrote Odell off for that day at least and addressed ourselves to the task presented by the steep scree. It was not as loose as scree can be, but it was loose enough to make it very hard work for the man in front, whose feet sank down several inches at every step. We rejoiced to see a stream of water coming down, indicating that we might find water on top of the ridge. We had had some doubt about this and later it was disappointing to see that the source of this stream was a good 500 ft. below the crest.

It took over two hours to climb the 1500 ft. to the top, and, before it was reached, rain, which presently turned to snòw, began to fall. We gained the crest at a notch just below the fantastically weathered 'coxcomb' of crumbling yellow rock which gave the ridge its serrated appearance and also its name, for we now preferred the 'Coxcomb', *tout court*, to the former 'Saw-tooth' or 'Serrated' ridge.

Where we stood the ridge runs roughly east and west. On the south side, up which we had come, is the South-East glacier, one branch of which flows round the eastern foot of the ridge from its head beneath the southern slopes of East Nanda Devi, Nanda Devi itself, and the mile of snow ridge connecting the two. These slopes, together with the south ridge of Nanda Devi, make up a tremendous cwm, comparable, though on a lesser scale, to the West Cwm of Everest. From our position on the ridge then it will be understood that we looked down on to the upper névé of the South-East glacier and across it to East Nanda Devi. Had our erratic (I use the word in its strict sense of 'wandering') scientist continued his course up the right bank of the glacier, we would now have seen him on the glacier below us; but this we neither hoped nor expected, and I mention it merely in an attempt to explain the topography.

We now turned west along the crest of the ridge until driven off it by the steep and jagged rocks, below which we traversed on the north side. There was no sign of water, nor did it appear likely that we should find any higher up. The only alternatives for a base camp were on the névé of the glacier 200 or 300 ft. below us or near the source of the stream which we passed on the way up. The former would have been a fairly frigid spot for a base camp and the presence of water was problematical; the advantages were its height and the fact that the whole of our proposed route up the mountain would be in view. On the south side of the ridge the camp would be on shale, which is as preferable to ice for sleeping on as a feather bed is to a 'donkey's breakfast'. Also water was plentiful; but against this was the 500 ft. plug up to the ridge

South face of Nanda Devi from South glacier;
route follows ridge running diagonally across face

and the fact that the mountain would not be in view at all, though some of us thought this was a point in its favour. Emmons was the only one who preferred the glacier site. As he would have to spend most of his time there his opinion carried weight, but he was overruled, and I hope he was duly grateful.

While this discussion was going on, we were getting colder and wetter, so we dumped the loads under the 'Coxcomb' wall, covered them up, and hurried back. These loads contained nothing that we could not do without at the base, and we could therefore leave them here to be picked up when we returned this way to establish Camp I. Plunging and scree-riding down the southern slope, we reached the bottom in about twenty minutes, where we found a note from Odell saying that he had left his load and gone back to camp.

We followed him there, arriving at half-past three, and were mightily surprised to find Carter. We had calculated that he could not get here for another two days and I am afraid our first reaction was a feeling of relief that the Apricot Brandy had been drunk last night. Kalu was with him, his damaged reputation somewhat mended, and two other coolies, one from Mana and one from Lata—an acquisition of strength which would have been more welcome had we not got to feed them. The Bhotias got back later with big loads of wood.

The morning of the 6th was as unpleasant as it could be, raw, wet, and misty. The Sherpas, less Da Namgyal, and the Sahibs, got away with loads by nine o'clock, but the Bhotias were extremely reluctant to leave their tents. They disliked the glacier travel and made anxious inquiries about the route, but luckily I was able to assure them that it was free from ice or snow. Even so, much patience was required, but at last, an hour later, they made up their loads of fuel and started. Da Namgyal remained in camp because his cough was troubling him. He had suffered from this almost from the start and every night we would hear him coughing in the most distressing way; he must have made sleep difficult for his tent-mates, who were probably relieved when I sent him down.

The Mana men needed coaxing on the way up and I was fearful lest they should jib; indeed on one occasion when I had got too far ahead they were so long in coming that I went back to look for them, fully expecting to find that they had had enough. However, they

The South-East glacier and part of the Basin wall

brightened up when we reached the scree slope and I could point out our destination, nor were they long in reaching it. We were joined here by Odell, who had retrieved yesterday's error and was now carrying two loads. The others passed us on the way down, but by three o'clock the last of us were back at the Moraine Camp, having dumped the loads and the wood on a fairly flat site close to the highest water. Into the remainder of the short afternoon we crowded the writing of letters and the further weeding out of our kits, for tomorrow the Base Camp would be occupied and the Mana men dismissed.

A wonderfully fine morning greeted us on this important day. On account of the Mana men there was no time to waste since they had to carry loads to the Base Camp, receive their pay, and then get down to the wood and warmth of Sanctuary Camp because they would be without tents.

More kit was left here, things that we should not need on the mountain and things that never should have been brought. Odell and I had some harsh words over the glacier drill, because in making up the loads for the men this had been left out on the assumption that it would stay here, an erroneous assumption, because we now learnt that what to our uninstructed minds appeared to be a perfectly good bit of glacier was to the scientific mind beneath contempt. The glacier down here was too old, worn, and decrepit to yield the desired results; its temperature at depth—'the be-all and the end-all' of our hopes, the sum of our ambition, that which we had left England to find—this could only be taken where it was young, fresh, and unsullied by a covering of stones. The glacier drill went with us.

We made good time and reached the new camp at half-past eleven and immediately began paying off all the men, except Kalu, who was to stay with us in place of Da Namgyal, whose job was to go back with the Bhotias as far as Joshimath, where he could have a week or ten days' rest. Then having collected six men from Lata village he was to return up the gorge, bringing our mail and two loads of coolie food, and to arrive at the Base Camp by September 1st.

Kalu was overjoyed at being promoted to the ranks of the Sherpas, though I take leave to doubt whether the joy was mutual. He indulged in a little of his customary chest-thumping but retained sufficient presence of mind to claim Da Namgyal's high-altitude

The Base Camp

Nima Tsering

clothing and boots, which Da Namgyal was very loth to surrender. That important point settled in his favour, Kalu then made the round of the Sahibs, praying diligently, and cadging tobacco. He was the most inveterate smoker I have ever met and would smoke charcoal, paper, or old rags if there was nothing else. Now that the Mana men were leaving he was without a pipe, but he got over that in a very ingenious manner. He made a long sloping hole in the earth like the adit of a miniature mine, and then sank a vertical shaft to cut this at the lower end. The shaft was filled with tobacco, or in Kalu's case anything inflammable, and the smoker's mouth was applied to the mouth of the adit. It gives, I imagine, a very cool smoke, and does away with the tiresome necessity of carrying a pipe about, and to this day I regret that I did not get Kalu to try the same method during his very brief residence on snow.

The paying off of the Mana men took place under circumstances very different to the last pay-day, even if only because it was a fine hot day instead of a pouring wet one. These men had done all, and more, than was expected of them. We could be liberal ungrudgingly, and we parted, at any rate on our side, with feelings of esteem and almost affection. They are the most likeable of men and in character not unlike the Sherpas; given the opportunity, they might in time become as useful on a mountain as the Sherpas, but if that was ever the case I should hate to have the paying of them. For once they now appeared satisfied with what we gave them, true they asked for more, but only as a matter of form, and the demand was not pressed very hard. Many and profound were their salaams, and then they ran down the scree, laughing and shouting like schoolboys on a holiday. To them we owed a lot.

It was a great satisfaction to be here. We felt that at last after nearly a month, or in some cases two months, of preparatory drudgery the stage was set and the supernumeraries dismissed; or, like a builder who, having finished the prosaic task of digging the foundations, was about to begin the more exciting job of erecting the walls. To be rid of all coolies and to have no one but the Sherpas and ourselves to look after gave a new feeling of confidence, for, capable though the Bhotias are of taking care of themselves, they can yet be a source of worry. It is one of the drawbacks of Himalayan climbing that coolies should be necessary, but I think that anyone who has travelled with the better type of Sherpa would like to have them along with him whether necessary or not, just for the fun of their companionship.

We had good reason to be pleased with the result of all this preliminary work. We were not more than a week behind schedule, we had a comfortable Base Camp stocked with a month's food and three weeks' wood fuel, and everybody except two of the Sherpas was in good health and spirits. None of us had had any sickness on the way up, apart from a few septic sores. Loomis was the worst sufferer in this respect, but his were now practically healed, thanks to Houston's assiduous attention.

There were too many unknown factors for us to gauge with any accuracy our chances of getting to the top, but at this stage we were decidedly hopeful. The view of the south ridge from Pisgah had rather dashed us, but a closer, though fleeting, look from the 'Coxcomb' ridge *en face*, even with due allowance for foreshortening, had been encouraging. But if the first appearance had proved to be false, common sense might have told us that the other need not be true. That this was so we were presently to learn.

CHAPTER XIII

A FIRST FOOTING

I HAVE ALWAYS ADMIRED those people who before ever reaching a mountain, perhaps even before seeing it, will draw up a sort of itinerary of the journey from base camp to summit—a complicated affair of dates, camps, loads, and men, showing at any given moment precisely where A is expected to be, what B will be doing, what C has had for breakfast, and what D has got in his load. It always reminds me of the battle plans an omniscient staff used to arrange for us in France, where the artillery barrage and the infantry went forward, hand in hand as it were, regardless of the fact that while there was nothing whatever to impede the progress of the barrage, there were several unknown quantities, such as mud, wire, and Germans, to hamper the movements of the infantry.

Parallels drawn from warfare are apt, and difficult to avoid, but they assort very ill with the spirit of mountain climbing; yet any programme that includes a human factor is liable to go amiss, and in our case almost every factor was unknown. Moses himself, who was no mean organiser, could hardly cope with a problem of movement which included such imponderables as the route, the state of the snow, the rate of climbing, the weather, the porters, and the powers of acclimatisation of a party only two of which had been over 17,300 ft. before.

In the final stages of a climb, when the unknowns have been greatly reduced, a time-table is essential, but we made no attempt to elaborate any such miracle of organisation and foresight at this early hour. We might have succeeded in keeping in step for one day, but, as will appear, the second and third days would have played the devil with it.

The first thing to do was to find a Camp I and take up everything we should need on the mountain, including food for twenty-five days, leaving at the Base Camp a week's extra food and twenty days' food for Emmons, who was stopping there. We had the advantage of knowing that there were no difficulties up to 19,000 ft., so we were able to start without waiting to reconnoitre. We completed our loads from the dump on the ridge and continued traversing below the 'Coxcomb', the Sherpas carrying 60 lb. and ourselves 40 lb., which we found was as much as we could well manage at this height.

We kept as high as possible under the rock wall, over some very loose ground, and as soon as the ridge beyond the 'Coxcomb' looked feasible we edged up to the left to get on to it. To do this a patch of snow had to be crossed, but even at the late hour of midday it was in fair condition, a fact we noted with premature satisfaction. On the crest of the ridge we were once more on rock and at one o'clock we reckoned the height at 19,000 ft. This was gauged by taking a clinometer reading to the top of what was known as 'Longstaff's Col', a col on the rim of the Basin at the foot of the shoulder of East Nanda Devi. It is not a pass, or at least it was not then, because it had not yet been crossed, but in 1905 Dr Longstaff and his two guides, the Brocherels, had stood on this col and were the first to look down into the inner Sanctuary. To quote Dr Longstaff: 'Below us was an extraordinary chaos of wind-driven cloud, half veiling the glaciers which surround the southern base of Nanda Devi. Above was the vast southern face of the great peak, its two summits connected by a saddle of more than a mile in length. From this spot the mountain strangely resembles Ushba, and the likeness must be even more striking from the West. Directly from the col rose the southern ridge of the eastern peak by which we hoped to make the ascent.'

By now none of us were feeling very strong and it was time to look for a camp site, for there was nothing suitable in the immediate vicinity. While we were admiring the view or, less euphemistically, resting, Houston and Loomis went up about 300 ft. and reported there was a possible site. When we got to it, it appeared so uninviting that I went up still higher, hoping to find something better. But there was not the vaguest suggestion of a tent platform, the rock of uniform steepness sloped away to the névé of the glacier on the one side, on the south was a precipice, and the ridge in between was too narrow and broken even to climb, much less furnish a platform. It now began to snow, so we fell furiously to digging out and building up three platforms on the proposed site. At the end of an hour's hard work, we had three passable platforms, one big enough for the two-man bivouac tent and two for the larger 6 ft. x 7 ft. tents. This done, we stowed the loads under a convenient ledge and hurried back to the Base Camp at half-past four. The height of this Camp I was 19,200 ft.

At breakfast next morning what may have been a spontaneous and was certainly an almost unanimous desire for an off-day found expression. It happened to be a Sunday, so we may have felt that some recognition of this was due, or perhaps a mental itinerary had persuaded us that we had more time in hand than would be needed to complete the job. It was so tempting to divide the remaining 6000 ft. into three lifts of 2000, allot a couple of days to each and one day to get down, and so climb the mountain in a week. Poor Maurice Wilson, who tried to climb Everest alone and died on the glacier of exhaustion, had much the same notion; but for him the problem was even simpler, for he did not worry much about height and estimated his task in terms of distance—a mere seven miles from Rongbuk monastery to the top.

A fine, sunny morning made some of us regret the waste of a good day, but a wet afternoon made amends. It may have been a wise resolve physiologically, but tactically it was a mistake, because experience shows that there are usually enough involuntary rest-days due to weather without adding any voluntary ones. The time was spent pleasantly enough smoking too much, eating too much, and in too much group-photography—the results of these alone, portraying as they do what looks like a blackguardly group of political refugees (politics according to taste), are ample condemnation of off-days. Loomis and Emmons relieved me of the catering for the day and I have grateful recollections of some inspired hominy cakes. The Sherpas had rigged up a very effective roof for the kitchen out of the big tarpaulin and the ponderous steel tent poles, which now almost justified their existence, but which, I am glad to say, were not to go any higher. We had three light aluminium poles for use on the mountain and, though they were fragile enough to look at, they stood up uncommonly well.

Early in the night the rain turned to snow and when we woke next morning there were six inches of snow at the camp, and the glacier below was white down to 14,000 ft. It was still snowing hard, so we sat tight and towards midday the wind got up and very soon a blizzard was blowing from the south-east. Conditions were rather miserable,

Camp I (19,200 ft.); peaks on southern rim at back

the kitchen roof blew away at intervals or collapsed under the weight of snow, and even when up afforded little protection to the fire or to anyone working there. To add to our worries Kitar and Nuri were now on the sick list. Nuri had never recovered from his attack at Pisgah and daily looked more fragile and more anxious; clearly we could strike him off the strength. Kitar had complained of his stomach at Pisgah, but after being dosed had said no more about it. I noticed he always took the lightest loads he could and we thought he was a bit of a 'lead-swinger', but in this we maligned him.

Meanwhile we lay in our tents thinking sorrowfully on sundials and their sententious advice about the passing moment and the lost day that never returns, and vowing with many oaths that we would go up to Camp I on the morrow, blizzard or no blizzard. It was still snow-ing and blowing in gusts when we turned out, but there were breaks in the flying scud and a brighter patch of light in the murky sky assured us that the sun had risen even if the cock had not crowed.

This day we meant to establish Camp I, but only ourselves were to sleep there, the Sherpas returning to the Base Camp and bringing up the final loads on the following day. The loads had to be dug out from under a canopy of snow and it was half-past nine before we began plodding heavily up to the ridge in the soft new snow. On the north side of the 'Coxcomb' the snow was deeper and we were forced to take a lower route, changing the lead every ten minutes. This route took us on to the névé of the glacier, where we had a sorry time floundering in soft snow, and were finally led into what appeared to be a bottomless pit. At this point there was some discussion whether we should keep down a little longer or at once strike up over the snow-covered rocks to the ridge. It seemed to me rather like debating the advisability of walking in the ditch or on the road, but the luckless man in the lead, although up to the neck in snow, still evinced a strange preference for the lower route. Pasang, however, who happened to be next, had no doubt about it and struck out boldly for the rocks, where the rest of us speedily followed. Our ruffled feelings caused by this ignominy soon recovered on the better going afforded by the ridge, and by two o'clock we had reached our goal.

The snow had stopped by now and the wind died away, but the diminutive platform buried under snow and the complete absence of any drips of water from the rocks formed a very discouraging welcome. All hands fell to clearing away the snow, and at almost the first dig one of our two precious Bernina shovels went down the *khud*. These Berninas are light collapsible shovels of aluminium which are invaluable for digging tent platforms in snow. The business end of this one was improperly secured and at the first thrust came off the handle, went over the edge of the platform, and so down the snow slope to the glacier 500 ft. below. This was the second, but neither the last nor the most aggravating, occasion on which we learnt that the laws of gravity were much the same on Nanda Devi as elsewhere.

Owing to the accident of the ground, the three platforms were of necessity at considerable intervals apart, and to pass from one to the other was quite a climb. The job of cooking was assigned to the middle tent, of which Odell and myself were the unlucky occupants, on the specious pretext that it was most handy. Our system of allotting tents was a haphazard one and the only guiding principle was that of frequent changes. The object of this was to avoid any tendency to form cliques and it was beneficial in various ways. If a man knows that his martyrdom has only to be endured for a night or two running, he can tolerate good-humouredly the queerest little idiosyncrasies of his stable companions. Some of us talked too much or too loudly, some did not talk enough, some smoked foul pipes, some ate raw onions, some never washed, some indulged in Cheyne-Stokes breathing, and one even indulged in Cheyne-Stokes snoring. I should explain that this form of respiration afflicts one at high altitudes and only occurs during unconsciousness. Short bursts of increasingly violent panting, as though the victim was suffocating, rise to a crescendo and are succeeded by complete stillness as if the man has died, although a quickly recurring spasm convinces the other occupants of the tent that this unfortunately is not so. The devastating effects of this sort of thing when combined with snoring can be imagined. But these singularities, which, if endured for too long, might lead to murder, were, by our system of musical chairs, matter only for frank criticism or even amusement.

The unfortunate necessity of cooking, from which we seem to have wandered, was on the mountain a very simple routine. All that it implied was boiling the porridge and beating up the dried milk in the morning, and in the evening boiling the pemmican. No more was allowed, and in the fullness of time (such is habit), no more was expected—I was going to say 'desired', but that perhaps would be putting it too strongly. It sounds simple enough, but the production of these sybaritic repasts needed first the presence of a Primus stove in the cook's tent. Moreover, this stove had to be lit and kept alight in the teeth of all the devils which seemed at once to take possession of it, causing it to splutter, smoke, lick the tent roof with a devouring flame, do everything in fact except burn. Perhaps I exaggerate, for all were not like this, the outbreaks were few, and with skilled and sympathetic handling need not occur at all. Still there the beastly thing was in the tent, room had to be made for it, patience exerted on it, the fingers burnt by it, the nostrils assailed by it, and its fumes swallowed. To have to do and suffer thus was excellent moral discipline, but it should only be taken in small doses and the stove should change tents as frequently as the personnel.

Cooking was only the penultimate duty of the cook; before this came the providing of water and after it the dishing out into seven expectant mugs—enamel ones that is. Here both skill and expedition were required, for if there was expedition and no skill the tent floor received the most liberal helping, and, if the converse held, the pemmican congealed before the other tents got their ration. Practice, as always, makes perfect, and it was astonishing what prodigies of pouring were performed from any height, at any angle, and, if need be, in the dark.

The provision of water was at Camp I a simple matter except on this first night when everything was under snow. Thereafter there was a useful drip from some nearby rocks and a cunning distribution of pots in the morning assured the evening supply. Higher up it was not so easy, and ice or hard snow had to be dug out in sufficient quantity. The melting of this takes longer than the boiling, and some judgment is needed to know what amount of water different types of snow will yield. The hapless cook lights his stove, puts the snow on to melt, and while this is doing takes off his boots and gets into his sleeping bag. He then discovers that a heaped saucepan of snow has yielded a teacupful of water, and perforce leaves his warm bag, puts on his boots, and collects more snow—not only in the saucepan but also in his imperfectly laced boots and socks. An attempt was made to enact that the tent doing the cooking should also distribute the food to the other tents, but this seemed to Odell and me (at that moment anyhow) a monstrous arrangement akin to sweated labour, or like making the condemned man dig his own grave.

Next morning was fine and cold but did not look promising. The party split up, three went down to the dump to help the Sherpas and were also commissioned to look for the shovel, Graham Brown and Houston were to prepare a fourth tent platform against the arrival of the Sherpas, and Odell and myself had the more interesting job of reconnoitring for the second camp. Immediately above us there appeared to be about 800 ft. of rock and snow ridge similar to that on which we were, and beyond was a steep snow arête, which continued for possibly 500 ft., before flattening out into a convenient snow saddle, the very place, we thought, for Camp II.

It was indeed the very place for a camp, but it was not Camp II that we put there but Camp III, and it was five days later before it was occupied.

How hopelessly out we were in these glib estimates, due to foreshortening, was apparent in a very short time, and henceforth we took very little on trust. For 700 or 800 ft. we mounted steadily, taking a line just below the crest of the ridge on the east side of it, for on the western it was precipitous. It was by no means similar to the ridge below, being decidedly steeper and very much looser. In fact when we came to carrying loads up here it became a nightmare owing to the danger from loose rocks, nor was it possible to escape the danger by keeping to the crest, so sharp and broken was it. If I am ever guilty of using the phrase 'firm as a rock' again, I shall think of this ridge and strike it out.

Above this horrible section the rocks were snow-covered and before going any farther we sat down for a long rest at what was subsequently known as the 'roping-up place', for from this point onwards a rope was essential. Both of us were feeling the effects of altitude here, though later in the day, when we got higher, we felt it less; perhaps we were taken out of ourselves by the more interesting and difficult climbing in the same way that a man will cease being sea-sick if the ship is sinking—having something better to think about. Between 19,000 ft. and 20,000 ft. seemed to be the critical height and both the old hands and the newcomers suffered from extreme lassitude, and one or two from headaches and slight nausea. Personally I was astonished at the speed with which those who had not been high before did acclimatise, and how comparatively mild their symptoms were. In 1935 four of us, crossing a pass of only 17,000 ft. from Sikkim into Tibet, suffered extremely, and although carrying no loads were quite incapable of keeping pace with our transport which, since it included some yaks, was not exactly devouring the ground. Such discrepancies are difficult to explain and a great deal has yet to be learnt about acclimatisation. Houston collected all the data he could to help in this object and persuaded most members of the party to submit to keeping a very detailed and indecently intimate record of their day-to-day symptoms and feelings. The keeping of such records in the cause of science is I suppose very praiseworthy, and since questions had to be answered and symptoms noted in that grim interval between awakening and getting out of one's sleeping bag, it showed amazing restraint and commendable determination in all who undertook the task. To be confronted morning after morning, at that unseasonable hour, with such questions as how one had slept, and what one at that moment most desired, would compel most people, including the writer, to try to be funny at the expense of truth. Psycho-analysis, medical examinations, oxygen masks, *et hoc genus omne*, seem a far cry from mountaineering as understood by Whymper, Leslie Stephen, Mummery and the giants of the past.

The effects of the recent blizzard were felt on this upper section, because there was a lot of fresh snow which had to be cleared away before steps could be cut in the underlying harder snow or ice. For some way it was a straightforward upward traverse just below or sometimes on the crest of the ridge, but presently a double cornice warned us off the crest just when this course had become most desirable owing to the increasing angle of the snow slope.

On one pitch the snow beneath the cornice was so steep and deep that, instead of steps, a continuous track had to be scraped and stamped out, and at the farther end of this critical passage a hole had to be flogged through another cornice, crowning a short lateral rib, which crossed our line at right angles. Having successfully emulated the camel, we were rewarded by a good stance, where one man could anchor the party with an axe belay while the other essayed a traverse across some rotten rocks, covered with snow and verglas. Thanks to a loose rock, the leader here came unstuck and shot down some distance before being stopped by the rope secured round the second's axe driven deeply into the snow.

After this, in every sense moving, incident we regained for a short space the security of the ridge only to be driven off again by a cornice under which another long traverse had to be made. Early in the day our ambitions had been fixed on the snow saddle; at the roping-up place the snow arête leading to it would have contented us; and, as the difficulties increased, so our hopes receded down the ridge, until now we were aiming at what looked like a rock platform, only 100 ft. above us and still 300 ft. from the foot of the arête. Even this we were destined not to see.

This last traverse took longer than we expected, because once more a continuous track had to be beaten out while the overhang of the cornice did its best to shove us off. By the time we had finished this, snow was falling, and it was three o'clock, so we decided to call it a day. We were probably 1500 ft. above Camp I and, considering the route, it was clear that this would be a long enough carry when laden. The fact that in all the distance we had come there was no suitable place for a tent was disturbing, but we had strong hopes of the top of the rock bulge now just above us.

We got down at five o'clock to find the others back and four Sherpas ensconced in the fourth tent. No Bernina shovel had been found and another similar accident had occurred. A full tin of tea, left on the platform outside one of the tents, had for some unexplained reason gone over the edge. The only witnesses to this tragedy were Graham Brown and Houston, who were working on another platform and suddenly noticed it rolling down the slope; and it was the more serious because, but for an ounce, this was all the tea we had left. I think that the only drink worth having on a mountain is one which will quench thirst, and that things like cocoa and patent drinks, which pretend to be food as well, are not worth their weight. After all, the bulk of the food, like pemmican and porridge, is slops and what is really wanted is something to eat, that is chew, and something to drink, not an anaemic mixture of the two. Even the Americans, traditionally hostile to tea and addicted to cocoa and kindred drinks, came round to this point of view and felt the deprivation as much as the tea-swilling British.

We were rather wet and miserable and by nightfall it was snowing hard, a state of affairs which gave us more concern on account of the lost tea than for its effect on the mountain; every flake that fell buried it deeper and lessened the already remote chances we had of finding it.

Lloyd and Carter were still feeling the altitude here and Kalu and Phuta were both sick, so they were detailed to go down and look for the tea. Four full-grown men poking about in the snow of a glacier for a 1 lb. tin of tea sounds like mountaineering with Alice in Wonderland, but it seemed natural enough at the time and it gives some measure of how we felt our loss. In a few days the Americans, who have not been brought up on tea, were talking about it as they might of whisky in the days of Prohibition, so that the hell of unfulfilled longing which the wretched Englishmen endured can well be imagined.

Five of us carrying 20 lb., and Pasang and Nima carrying 40 lb., set out to find Camp II. The 700 ft. up to the roping-up place were purgatorial, particularly for the leader, for the task of finding the best route and at the same time treading delicately, like Agag, to avoid launching great rocks on to those below was very wearing. The slightest mistake in placing a foot would inevitably send down a stone and a too vigorous use of the hands would have brought a large piece of the arête about one's ears. In places it was impossible to avoid crossing back above those behind, and the only thing to do was to wait until they were clear. I nearly bagged Odell this way, but he managed to duck and the rock went over his head.

At eleven o'clock it began snowing again. We climbed on two ropes of three and four, with a Sherpa in the middle of each, and by half-past one had reached almost to yesterday's highest point. The old steps were of great use, but all had to be cleared again of snow and, laden as we were, we moved with great caution, particularly on the traverse leading to the needle's eye, which was petrifying for the performer though probably amusing enough for the onlooker. At the thinnest part of the traverse a protruding ice bulge enforced the adoption of almost a crawl to get by, and, if the attitude was not sufficiently humble, the load jammed under the bulge, greatly to the embarrassment of its bearer

Camp II or the Gîte, 20,400 ft.

and the diversion of the second man who, fortunately, at this critical juncture, had a secure axe belay in a niche beneath the cornice.

Just before the upper traverse there was perhaps room for a small bivouac tent, so, leaving the others there in case nothing better was found, Odell and I crossed the traverse to investigate the platform which we had failed to reach the previous day. The movement round the projecting nose of rock covered with snow of doubtful integrity was a delicate one, but we were rewarded by finding on top of the nose a place which with a little work could be made to hold one tent, possibly two. It was a slightly sloping snow-covered ledge measuring about 6 ft. x 20 ft. set in the angle of a sheer rock wall, which enclosed it on two sides. On the third side was the way by which we had come and the fourth fell away steeply to the glacier now nearly 2000 ft. below. At first sight it looked as though we had entered a cul-de-sac, but a little search disclosed a snow ledge outside the rock wall furnishing an exit almost as perfunctory as the entrance.

It was now late, so without bringing the others up we dumped our two loads there and all went down together. We got back to Camp I wet through and found Emmons had come up to see what was happening. When he went down he took with him Kalu, the great chest-thumping Kalu who had already had enough— perhaps he wanted to get back to somewhere where he could dig holes in the ground for a pipe. The all-important matter of finding a place for Camp II had been settled and we had learnt that at any rate two of the Sherpas were fairly safe climbers. Pasang was particularly steady and Nima too was good but a bit light-hearted in his management of the rope. On the whole therefore it had been a day of gains, but against this was Kalu's defection, Phuta's sickness, the weather, and failure to find the tea. I must have been feeling a bit hipped myself, a state of mind which in politer society than that of our own we would have called 'sanguinary-minded', for the last entry in my diary runs: 'Still snowing 7 p.m. and we still cooking.'

CHAPTER XIV

ON THE MOUNTAIN

◆

O UR PLAN NOW WAS for two of us to occupy Camp II or the Gîte, as it was appropriately called, and on the following day, while those two went up higher to look for a Camp III, two Sherpas would join them at the Gîte. We assumed that a site for Camp III would be found on the snow saddle, and on the third day the Sherpas would assist in establishing the two Sahibs there while two more of us in turn occupied the Gîte.

It was a fine morning on the 14th, but we did not get away until 10 a.m. Graham Brown and Houston, who were going to sleep at Camp II, had to pack up the bivouac tent and their own gear and then someone dropped a mug down the *khud* and Houston very sportingly went down after it. The task looked hopeless in all the new snow, but he got it. Odell stayed in camp to catch up with his geological notes, but six of us started with Pasang and Nima.

At the roping-up place Carter went back as he had not yet acclimatised, and from there we climbed on three ropes, Lloyd and Nima, Pasang and myself, and Graham Brown, Houston, and Loomis. As usual the steps had to be cleared of snow and in places they were now not very reliable, but by cutting deep in they held sufficiently well. The passage round and up the projecting nose below the Gîte roused so much misgiving that we talked of putting a fixed rope there. But it was an awkward place to fix anything and in the end familiarity bred sufficient contempt for us to do without. A rope of two can move quicker than one of three, so Lloyd and I got there well ahead of the others and Pasang and Nima began making a platform; it now looked as though there would just be room for the bivouac tent and a big one. When they had finished I took them down on my rope, Lloyd waiting for the others, who had not yet arrived. By six o'clock it was snowing again.

The journey to Camp II, though now a daily routine, was never boring however unpleasant it might be in other ways. The unstable

147

rocks of the lower half still lay in wait to punish any carelessness, and on the upper section the daily snow-fall made it at least look like a new ascent.

The next day all started except Phuta and, when we reached the roping-up place, we descried what looked like two flies crawling up the steep snow arête above the Gîte. These of course were Graham Brown and Houston, and we watched them anxiously, making ribald remarks about their rate of progress and their frequent halts. The fact that we were ourselves sitting down eating chocolate by no means lessened our enjoyment of this spectacle and certainly increased the flow of wit. We felt like dramatic critics eating their chocolates in the stalls, and sharpened the pencils of our wit accordingly.

It was a fine day for a change and the bright sun on the snow sapped our energy. We were up by 2 p.m. and having seen the tent pitched, for which there was just room enough, and Pasang and Nima safely established there, Lloyd and I went down, while Odell and Loomis waited to hear the news from above. An hour later Graham Brown and Houston got back to Camp II, and reported that there were a couple of hundred feet of difficult climbing before the snow arête was reached, that this was steep and long, but that a good site for a camp had been found where the arête merged into the broad saddle. They had felt the sun even more severely than we had.

We got down to Camp I at four o'clock and Phuta requested that he might go to the Base Camp that evening. It was no use keeping him, so I gave him a chit to Emmons and sent him down. There were now five of us at Camp I, two Sahibs and two Sherpas at Camp II, and Emmons, Kalu, and three Sherpas at the Base Camp.

Next day, the 16th, two more Sahibs had to occupy Camp II, and at half-past nine we all started, Odell and I carrying our personal kit and some odds and ends. Some student of human nature has remarked that 'no one can do an act that is not morally wrong for the last time without feelings of regret', but now I was doing the climb from Camp I to Camp II for the fifth and last time and can very positively refute that statement. Of course devout Hindus might say that in climbing Nanda Devi we were committing an immoral act and that would account satisfactorily for my absence of regret.

Before reaching the roping-up place, we were bothered by seeing two tents still standing at the Gîte and it looked as though no move was in progress. Later we made out somebody on the arête but could see only two instead of the four we expected. We puzzled our heads over this and made many wild conjectures. If Graham Brown and Houston were not moving up to Camp III there would be some congestion at the Gîte, but Odell and I were determined to sleep there, even if it meant four in a tent. We could not face yet another ascent from Camp I.

It was no use speculating, and as Odell was going slowly, and I was not unwilling to do the same, he and I went along together while the other three pushed on as fast as they could to find out what the matter was. We two continued in leisurely fashion, not arriving until three o'clock. Perhaps we were carrying heavier loads; Odell certainly was, for he was cluttered up with hypsometers, clinometers, and thermometers, and was so attached to certain favourite but unnecessary articles of clothing that his personal kit was a portentous affair—nor was Da Namgyal there to carry it as he should have been. I remember particularly a hideous yellow sweater, a relic of the War, which weighed more than the five Shetland woollies carried by us all; and at the highest camp he produced a hat which none of us had ever seen before and which, I suppose, had some attributes peculiarly fitting it for wear at 24,000 ft.

The mystery of the two tents was solved by a note and the presence of both Sherpas. Nima was sick and Pasang was completely snow-blind. The note told us that they had gone up with food and kit and asked us to bring on the tent and their sleeping bags. Loomis and Lloyd had already left with these when we arrived and halfway up the snow arête they were met by Houston and Graham Brown. For these four it was a hard day.

Houston's note went on to say that the necessary dope for alleviating snow-blindness had been unaccountably left at Camp I, and suggested that strong tea should be tried in the interim. Tea was at a premium, for we were carefully conserving our solitary ounce for higher up, but we brewed some and did what we could for Pasang, who was in considerable pain. He was lying on his face in the tent and quite unable to open his eyes, but by forcing the lids apart we managed to get some tea in. This treatment was continued until the medicine arrived two days later, but had little effect; nor had the medicine either for that matter, and, though we did not then suspect it, Pasang was now out of the hunt.

It was not easily understood how he had managed to get such a severe attack. Yesterday had been very bright and sunny but no one noticed him with his glasses off, nor were these any different from Nima's which were perfectly efficient. While he was preparing the platform here, I noticed he was working without glasses and it must have been then that his eyes were affected, although the platform was in shadow and there was more rock than snow. But a rarefied atmosphere makes the light more dangerous in this respect and we read that on Everest in 1924 Norton was snow-blind merely from the glare off rocks. In 1930 Shipton and I climbed Kilimanjaro (19,700 ft.), and on snow near the summit we both took off our glasses to see where we were, for there was a thick mist and not a sign of the sun. Nevertheless that same night we both went snow-blind and suffered great pain, but in twenty-four hours it passed off without any treatment and this led me to think that Pasang's would do the same.

When Lloyd and Loomis returned, we agreed that they should please themselves whether they came up tomorrow with the little that was left at Camp I to bring. They would not be able to sleep here because Odell and I would still be in residence. Another tent, more food, and our own kits had to be carried to Camp III before we could move up, and for reasons of acclimatisation it was a sound plan to sleep two nights at a camp before going on to the next.

When they had gone, we took stock of our surroundings. These consisted of blank rock wall and thin air in equal proportions; there were about four feet of terra firma between the two tents and one could walk, without a rope, for about ten paces round the corner where the exit lay. All view of the ridge was cut off and only a little of it immediately below the Gîte was visible, but to the east a wide field of vision included East Nanda Devi, 'Longstaff's Col' now well below us, a great crescent of fluted ice wall on the rim to the south of it, and, beyond, the beautifully proportioned Nanda Kot. The height was about 20,400 ft.

Having brewed the tea for Pasang's eyes and drunk some ourselves, we tried to instil some life into Nima, who seemed very lugubrious and lethargic—in much the same frame of mind as a passenger in the last stages of sea-sickness, who having prayed long and earnestly

On the way to Camp II

At foot of snow arête above Camp II

for the ship to sink has almost abandoned hope that it will. I think they had not eaten since they got there, so we made him light his stove and cook some pemmican, which the Sherpas relish far more than we do. They were in the roomy 6 ft. x 7 ft. tent while we occupied the small bivouac tent vacated by Graham Brown and Houston, who had taken up one of the larger ones. We graciously allowed the Sherpas to remain in the enjoyment of their luxurious quarters, but this generosity will not be counted unto us for righteousness because the atmosphere in their tent was such that no tent at all would have been preferable.

I forget the exact dimensions of our tent, but it was very long and narrow and the two occupants lay, literally, cheek by jowl—that is if the human face has a jowl; or is it confined to pigs? It was admirably suited to Odell, who is also long and a bit narrow, and I think this was the first night that he was able to lie at full length since he had left Ranikhet. On this expedition we were experimenting with air beds as insulation when lying on snow, instead of the usual rubber mats, half an inch thick and 3 ft. x 4 ft. The extra room they took up was very noticeable in a small tent and apart from that they were not altogether successful. Punctures were numerous and unless they amounted to bursts, as they sometimes did, they were not easy to locate; situated as we were, the method of plunging them into a bath and watching for bubbles was seldom practicable. If your bed did go flat, it was a serious matter because no protection at all was afforded, and the result was a cold and sleepless night. Again, if you blew them up too hard you rolled off, and if they were too soft you were in contact with the ground and therefore cold. The Sherpas used to blow them up as if they were blowing up a dying fire, with the result that one bounded about like a pea on a drum, and if two people sat on it when in that state the whole thing exploded. Pasang got a lot of amusement out of the operation of blowing up and deflating beds by making them produce discordant noises like ill-played bagpipes. Now that only two of the Sherpas were left, and those two incapable of raising even a zephyr, we had to blow our own up, and this process provided yet another example of the perfection of natural laws which can even legislate for the remote association of a mountaineer and an air bed; as we gained in altitude and lost breath, the beds required less air to fill them owing of course to the diminution of pressure.

There was a storm in the night but, packed as we were, it was easy to keep warm and difficult to keep cool. Pasang was still blind and very sorry for himself, but Nima was brighter and offered to come with us to Camp III. Odell and I took a tent and paraffin, and Nima 40 lb. of sugar. Care was required on a short stretch above the camp and an upward traverse on rather shaky snow took us on to the ridge. We left it again where it suddenly stood on end and got into trouble on the rocks which would, when climbed, bring us out above this steep bit which had so frightened us. Odell led over a steep ice-glazed traverse which Nima and I resolved mentally to have nothing to do with, and when he was securely placed we had ourselves more or less pulled up in a direct line.

We were now at the foot of the steep snow arête which was such a prominent feature from below, and we settled down to kicking steps up it very slowly and methodically, the steps made by our forerunners having vanished. It was a narrow ridge, but we were able to stick to the crest, or slightly on the Rishi side, which was now less steep than the east side, though both fell away sharply, and the upward angle was 40 or 45 degrees; it will be remembered that from Camp I to Camp II the route lay always on the east flank and that the Rishi side was a precipice. As might be expected after the persistent falls of the last week, there was a lot of fresh snow to kick through before solid footing was obtained, and when we reached the tent at Camp III Graham Brown told us exactly how many of these steps we had kicked out, he having counted them. As far as I remember, the figure was disappointingly small for we felt that it must be something astronomical, but in sober fact there were only about 700 ft. of snow ridge. Approaching the tent, the angle eased off and we found it pitched snugly under the shelter of a steep snow bank.

It was after midday, but Graham Brown and Houston were still in bed and evidently intended 'lying at earth' after their efforts of yesterday. Going back we rattled down in an hour, and this time reversed our upwards procedure by descending the very steep snow patch in order to avoid the rocks. Nobody had come up from below, Pasang was still blind, we both had slight headaches, it was snowing again, and there was a big sun halo; but all this was forgotten in the warm glow of self-righteousness induced by our virtuous activity.

Having thus acquired enough merit for the time being by working while others slept, we sat about next morning until Graham Brown and Houston came down from Camp III for more loads. We found it such a pleasant occupation that we sat about some more until the other three came up from Camp I. As soon as the first man's head appeared round the corner of the bulge below us, a shout went up to know if they had found the tea. They had no tea, but they brought the zinc-sulphate medicine and we now hoped that Pasang's recovery would be speedy; at present his eyes were as firmly closed as ever. Nima too had relapsed into his former state of misery, but even yet we did not despair of getting some useful work out of these two. There was still a load to come up from Camp I, so it was arranged that Carter and Nima should go down to-morrow for this and as much more food as they could carry.

At three o'clock four of us started back for Camp III, Odell and Houston on one rope, Graham Brown and myself on the other. We had the advantage of the steps made by them on the way down and, in spite of heavy loads, were up in two hours. Our tent platform was ready for us, so the others had not been so idle yesterday as we thought, and it was pleasant to have some room again, room outside as well as in. I was sorry we had not got a cat to swing.

As Odell and I lay that night with our cheeks and our jowls at a reasonable distance apart, we wondered happily whether the three below were suffocating in the bivouac tent or succumbing to asphyxiation in the overripe atmosphere of the Sherpas.

We flattered ourselves that the height of this camp was about 21,500 ft. but, if it was, it seemed highly improbable that from here we could put a bivouac within striking distance of the summit. It postulated a carry of 2000 ft. at the very least, 2500 would be better, and on the difficult going below we had not done a carry of more than 1500. The climbing was likely to get harder rather than easier and, of course, the increasing altitude would slow us up progressively. Repeated trials with the hypsometer made things appear even more discouraging by giving Camp III a height of only 21,200 ft., and though we knew by now that this instrument was, to put it mildly, subject to error, we had perforce to accept the lower figure in making future plans.

The question of the height of our camps bothered us a lot and, quite early on, the hypsometer had earned for itself an opprobrious

Camp III, 21,200 ft.

name of a like sound which may not be printed. For some reason or other we omitted to bring an aneroid barometer graduated for reading height; possibly our numerous scientists scorned an instrument which even the half-wits of the party could read. I remember in 1934 Shipton and I, having no scientific training, took with us an aneroid barometer out of an aeroplane. I think it cost ten shillings at one of those miscellaneous junk shops in Holborn. Our Sherpas conceived a great affection for it and called it 'Shaitan', probably because we consulted it so frequently. It worked very well until we dropped it. But this hypsometer, or boiling-point thermometer, while not giving us any very precise information, afforded everyone a lot of fun and the scientists food for thought. The results it gave were always interesting, sometimes amusing, and seldom accurate. For example, after several hours of exhausting climbing in what we foolishly thought was an upward direction, it was startling to learn that we had in reality descended a hundred feet from where we started. The learned scientists explained with bland assurance that such vagaries were to be expected, and were accounted for quite simply by the presence of a 'column of cold air'; the unlearned oafs on the contrary thought that it must be something to do with 'hot air', and plenty of it.

But there is generally some use to be found for the most unlikely things, and so it was with the hypsometer. It had as part of its equipment a small bottle of methylated spirits, and when we ran out of solid methylated for priming the stoves, this came in very handy. Priming a stove with paraffin is both noisome and inefficient.

On the 19th Graham Brown and Houston went down again to Camp II for loads while Odell and I went to spy out the land higher up. At the point we had reached, our ridge had widened out into a great hog's-back, so wide that it was in reality the south face, though up the middle of this face a ridge was still discernible, and 1000 ft. higher up it again stood out prominently. We struck straight up the middle of the face over what we called the 'snow saddle', avoiding the steep bank above the camp by a short traverse to the left. The snow was in good condition and the angle of slope about 30 degrees for the first 700 ft., after which it began to steepen. Above this was a sort of glacis of snow-covered rock lying at an angle of 45 to 50 degrees. In the steep places outcrops of rock appeared through the snow. This broad glacis

appeared to stretch upward for 1000 ft. until it narrowed again to a
sharp ridge. On our immediate right was a forbidding gully, a trap for
falling stones and ice, and beyond that the tremendous cirque which
forms the connecting ridge between East Nanda Devi and Nanda Devi
itself. Some two or three hundred yards to the left was a wide shallow
depression, scarcely a gully, and on the far side of it the horizon was
bounded by a very bold and steep ridge, probably the same which we
had looked at from Pisgah.

We attacked the glacis in the centre and worked upwards and to
the left, making for what looked like a slight ridge overlooking the
shallow gully. As we mounted, the angle grew steeper and the climbing
more difficult. At first a good covering of snow overlay the rocks, but
presently this became thinner and the outcrops of rocks more numerous. For mountaineering as well as geological reasons we were keenly
interested to reach the first of these outcrops, for the line we should
take, and our progress, depended greatly upon its quality. We hoped
that at this height it might have changed to something more honest
than the treacherous rock of the lower ridge, and that the strata might
lie in a more favourable direction. Technically it may have differed, but
for a climber it was substantially the same crumbling yellow stuff upon
which no reliance could be placed, and, though the dip of the strata
was now more in our favour, little comfort was to be derived from that
on rock of such rottenness.

When we had climbed about 500 ft. from the foot of the glacis, it
became apparent that the supposed ridge we were making for was no
ridge at all. To go straight up was still possible, but with loads on it
would be both difficult and dangerous, for nowhere was there enough
snow for an anchorage with an axe, or any rock round which a rope
could be belayed. We decided to traverse to the left and go for the shallow gully which appeared to offer a safe route on snow for at least 1000
ft. But shortly after putting this resolve into practice, we contrived to
get ourselves into such a mess on the ice-glazed face of a rock outcrop
that all our attention was concentrated on getting out of it, and instead
of continuing the traverse to the left we were compelled to embark
upon a long and tricky traverse in the opposite direction. By sticking
wherever possible to snow, and avoiding any rock like the plague, we
worried a way back down the glacis until we rejoined our earlier track.

A lower route was obviously the best line for the gully, but it was now too late for any more and we hurried back to camp, where we arrived in time to avoid the start of a blizzard. Two days had elapsed since the warning of the sun halo.

Lloyd and Loomis had come up here to sleep after only one night at Camp II in defiance of our self-imposed rule of two at each camp. No one, however, with experience of the Gîte would doubt their wisdom in making that camp an exception to the rule.

The results of our reconnaissance were mainly negative but not without value. It was clear that a route directly up the glacis should only be tried as a last desperate resource, and also that whichever way we went it was going to be a painfully long carry before a place where a tent could be pitched would be found. The conclusions were that further reconnaissance was needed, that the most promising line was the broad gully, and that in any case it would be advantageous to move the present camp to a new site at the foot of the glacis.

CHAPTER XV

ALARMS AND EXCURSIONS

◆

T HE NIGHT WAS COLD AND WINDY and no one turned out until nine o'clock. Lloyd and Loomis started out to have a look at the way to the gully, and the rest of us went down to Camp II for loads. All the tracks down had to be remade after the blizzard and we had long ceased to expect any tracks to last for twenty-four hours. To anticipate, they did not last so long to-day, and when we returned in the afternoon all were once more obliterated.

We found Pasang still blind and Nima not well, and it was pretty clear that neither would be any use. Nima's single journey to Camp III, the highest reached by any of the porters, was but a dying kick. The almost total failure of the Sherpas is easily explained, for, as I have pointed out, we had to take the leavings of several other expeditions. The only two I expected to go high were Pasang and Kitar. Of the others three were past their best and one was too young and inexperienced. Pasang of course was unlucky to be struck down with snow-blindness, but it cannot be said that it was not his own fault. Kitar was a victim to disease.

The medicine seemed to be having little effect on Pasang's eyes, and Nima's cheery grin was a thing of the past. That they should both go down was now the best course, but this was not possible until Pasang could see something. Apart from their rather miserable mode of existence at the Gîte, I was anxious to have them safely down at the Base Camp before we lost touch with them entirely by going higher up the mountain. We left them there, alone now, in the big tent, having told them that two of us would come down again to-morrow, and we started back, Carter with us, taking the small bivouac tent. Carter had a note which he had found at Camp I telling us that Emmons had moved the Base Camp down to the foot of the scree slope and that he was busy with the plane table, but only Kalu was able to help him by carrying loads.

It was cold and windy when we reached Camp III in a flurry of snow. There was a halo round the sun and two mock* suns, and I have seldom seen a more ominous-looking sky. The report of the reconnoitring party was more cheering than the weather. Taking a line below and to the left of ours, they had reached a point from where they could see into and up the gully. They had not got into it, but they reported that it could be reached by a route which lay almost entirely on snow, and that the going up the near side of it looked straightforward enough. Like us, they had seen no promise of a camp site higher up, and it was agreed to move this camp to the top of the snow saddle and to press the attack by the gully.

It was a quiet night in spite of all the signs of approaching storm, but the morning of the 21st dawned dull, misty, and snowy. We had a late breakfast and spent the morning in one tent discussing ways and means. Now that the thing was to be put to the test, it was clear that some difficult decisions would have to be made, and the upshot of our talk was that the responsibility for these decisions was put upon the writer. The too frequent use of the word 'I' in this narrative will not have escaped the notice of the reader. The reason for this is that up to now I may have had most to say in our affairs; but that was merely through the accident of my being the only one who knew the country or the porters. We had no official leader, and managed very well without, until at this crisis the need was felt for some kind of figurehead.

After a cup of cocoa additional to our lunch which, by the way, was usually a slab of chocolate and nothing else, Lloyd, Carter, and I went down again to Camp II for more loads, and the others took a first instalment of loads up to what would presently be Camp IV.

Pasang and Nima still appeared to be immovable, but I told them that two of us would come down again tomorrow and see them safely over the worst of the route to Camp I. Until they were down they were merely a source of anxiety, and, after to-morrow, we expected to be out of reach. We climbed up again in one and a quarter hours and it was

---

*   Mock suns are coloured images of the sun which appear on either side of the sun and at the same altitude. They probably result from the intersection of two halos and are fairly common in high latitudes.

Sunset—Camp IV and peak of East Nanda Devi

satisfactory to see that our time on the snow arête became faster, indicating that we were still acclimatising and not deteriorating. The other party had found a good camp site on the snow saddle near the foot of the glacis, and had dug out one tent platform.

The sunset was again threatening, with greasy-looking cigar-shaped clouds hanging low over East Nanda Devi, a greenish watery haze to the west, and, to the south, black banks of cumulus tinged with copper.

We woke to find the tent shaking and banging to the blasts of a fierce blizzard. The wind was coming out of the south-east, some snow was falling, but it was impossible to tell what was new snow and what was drift, for outside was nothing but a whirling cloud of driving snow. The three tents were close together and guyed to each other for mutual support. Six of us occupied the two big ones and Carter was by himself (a doubtful privilege under these conditions) in the small bivouac tent, pitched on the weather side. Odell, Lloyd, and I held the baby in the shape of the Primus stove, but it was conceivable that the inconvenience of fetching ice and breathing paraffin fumes was outweighed by the advantage of getting the food hot without having to fetch it. Going from the comparative warmth of the sleeping bag and the tent out into the blizzard was a breathtaking experience. Breathing was almost impossible facing the wind and nothing could be handled without mittens, while the act of leaving or entering the tent by the small sleeve entrance required the quick co-operation of all, unless the inside was to be covered with a layer of snow.

There was nothing to be done but lie in our bags, with one eye on a book and the other on the furiously flapping fabric and the quivering tent pole. The pole was of very light aluminium and we were rather nervous about it, but it stood the strain well, as did the tents, for which we forgave them all our past discomforts. At five o'clock, when we cooked our evening pemmican, conditions were unchanged. The wind still maintained a steady roar with occasional gusts of gale force, and we discussed the advisability of sleeping with windproofs on in case the tent went in the night. However, we pinned our faith to the fabric and did not resort to these extreme measures.

Morning brought no change in these unpleasant conditions, and we wondered whether it was blowing as hard at the Gîte and how the

Camp III after the blizzard, August 25th

Sherpas were faring. Anyhow, with the direction of the wind as it was, the rock wall would stop them being blown off their ledge.

The snow was being blown away as soon as it fell, and round our tent it had not accumulated to any great depth. The other big tent had not fared so well and there was a high bank of snow around it by morning. The pressure of this snow had reduced the space inside by half, so that the unfortunate residents were sleeping almost on top of each other. They had the consolation of knowing that their tent was now securely anchored. Carter too, in the bivouac, was experiencing trouble in keeping the snow-laden walls off his face.

Another weary day of inactivity and torpor passed, but towards evening the wind began to moderate and we were able to get outside, clear the accumulated snow away from the doors, and attend to the guys. Snow was still falling lightly and a leaden pall hid everything but the snow at our feet and three forlorn-looking tents.

Followed another cold and stormy night, but the morning of Monday the 24th dawned fine, calm and sunny. Had it been black as night, we would not have complained, for stillness was all we asked for after the battering of the last two days. The loss of this valuable time was disturbing, and though it may seem strange that two days in bed could be anything but beneficial, there was no doubt that the strain and the inaction had done us harm physically. Nor could we tell what effect the blizzard might have had on the snow of the upper slopes. It was imperative now to push on with all speed, and surely after such a snorter we might expect several days of fine weather.

These blizzards which we experienced, three of them lasting for thirty-six, twelve, and forty-eight hours respectively, all came from between east and south-east. Monsoon weather in the hills generally comes from between south and west, but these storms may have been deflected by the mountain. Such blizzards are more to be expected prior to the break of the monsoon, and during two previous monsoon periods in the Himalaya, one in Garhwal and one in the Everest region, I do not recollect one of any severity. This year the monsoon broke early and ended late, and was exceptionally severe in the United Provinces and Garhwal.

At nine o'clock Lloyd and I started out for Camp II in accordance with our promise to the Sherpas, the fulfilment of which the blizzard had compelled us to postpone. We left to the others the cold work of breaking out the tents from their frozen covering and digging out the buried stores, preparatory to carrying one big tent and the bivouac to the new Camp IV site. Five of us were to sleep up there to-night in readiness for carrying up a bivouac for the first summit party next day.

The presence of a lot of powder snow made conditions on the arête bad, and we both felt weak and got progressively weaker as we descended. Arrived at the Gîte, we were surprised to find it empty; evidently the Sherpas had tired of waiting for us and left early. It was comforting to know that the tent had weathered the storm, that Pasang's eyes must be better, and that we ourselves had not to descend any farther. Indeed, we were now in such a state of languor that our chief concern was how on earth we were going to get up again. We lolled about on the ledge, assailed by a violent thirst, feeling complete moral and physical wrecks; and it was evident that two days and nights in our sleeping bags had taken more out of us than a really hard day's work.

The Sherpas had taken the stove and cooking pot with them, but there was some food here and we opened a tin with an ice-axe—not for the sake of the food but for the tin, in which to catch the elusive drips from the rock wall. We had to sleep at the higher camp that night, so at midday we summoned up all our resolution and, taking with us all the food that was left here, we crawled weakly away from the Gîte.

I should be ashamed to say how long it took us to get back to Camp III, but by the time we arrived we were feeling better and our strength was beginning to return. Graham Brown and Carter, who were spending the night here, came down from Camp IV just as we arrived and informed us that up there it was perishing cold. Carter thought his toes were slightly touched with frost-bite.

Adding some more food to our loads, Lloyd and I went off once more and an hour of steady plodding brought us to the new camp. They had evidently started late that morning owing to the frozen tents, and, when we got up, the second tent was just being pitched. There was a bitter wind blowing and Loomis was inside attending to his feet, which also had been slightly affected by cold.

In spite of the cold, it was difficult to turn away from the astonishing picture painted by the fast-sinking sun. Nanda Kot still shone with dazzling purity like an opal, and beyond to the east was range upon range of the snow peaks of Nepal, looking like rollers breaking in white foam on a sunny sea. From the snow slope falling away out of sight at our feet, the eye swept across a great void till arrested by the castellated ivory wall of the Sanctuary, dominated by Trisul, up which the shadows were already stealing. And to the west was the dark chasm of the Rishi gorge, the clear-cut outline of the 'Curtain', and the blue-green swell of the foothills.

The height of Camp IV we estimated to be 21,800 ft., and with five of us here and food for nearly a fortnight we were in a strong position. If we could push a bivouac up another 2000 ft., the summit would be within reach, and, big 'if' though this was, the time had come to make the attempt. Of the five now at this camp, it was not difficult to decide which two should have the privilege of first shot. Odell was going very well and his experience, combined with Houston's energy, would make a strong pair. Assuming that we could place the bivouac high enough to-morrow, they were to have two days in which to make their attempt, and on the third day a second pair would take their place, whether they had been successful or not. The form shown to-morrow would indicate which two would have the second chance, and, provided the weather held, it might be possible to send up a third pair.

The 25th broke fine, but it was ten o'clock before we had made up our loads of 15 lb. each, which included food for two men for six days. During the blizzard, not very much snow had actually settled, and since then sufficient time had elapsed for this new snow to con-solidate. We found it in good condition. After gaining some height by kicking steps, we approached the gully by a long traverse where steps had to be cut and great care exercised. The snow covering grew thinner and we came to an uncomfortable halt on the steep lip of a minor hollow, cutting us off from the main gully. This was the far-thest point reached by Lloyd and Loomis, and they had seen that this difficult little gully could be avoided by working round the head of it, 200 ft. higher.

We sat here for a little, but it was no place for a long sojourn with-out prehensile trousers. There was not enough snow to afford a step, much less a seat, and the angle of the rock was such that mere friction was of no avail—boots, hands, and ice-axe were all needed to prevent

Loading up at Camp IV (21,800 ft.), Kedarnath peaks beyond

the beginning of a long slither which would only end on the glacier 6000 ft. below. Turning up the slope, the next few feet were of the same precarious nature that Odell and I had experienced on the glacis, but this was as yet the only part of the route where we had to forsake the security of the snow for the uncertainty of the rock. Once over this, we settled down to a long steady grind, kicking and cutting our way up very steep snow, and having rounded the head of this minor hollow, we took a line up the true left bank of the broad gully.

We were climbing on two ropes, so by changing the leading rope and also the leading end of each rope, the work was divided among four. It was a beautiful day, but in our perverse way we were not content, and were captious enough to wish the sun obscured so that we could climb in more comfort. Nanda Kot, 22,500 ft., sank below us and we began to cast jealous eyes on Trisul, which still looked down upon us majestically from its height of 23,400 ft. Meantime we began to search the snow above us for the slightest break in the relentless angle of the slope which might afford a site for a tent. We were tempted momentarily by the broken outline of the skyline ridge away across the gully, but we decided it was too far off and the approach to it too steep.

As we gained height, the curve of the face to our right grew rounder and narrower and the central ridge was beginning to stand out again like the bridge of a Roman nose. We edged over towards it, thinking that the rocks might provide easier going than the snow, and aiming for the foot of a rock tower where there might be a platform. Knowing by now the sort of rock we might expect, it was curious that we should so think, but such was the distorting effect on our minds of five hours of laborious step-kicking. The change of course was for the worse and we had some awkward moments before we dragged ourselves to the foot of the tower, to find it sloping away as steeply as the rest of the mountain.

The time was now three o'clock and our height something over 23,000 ft., practically level with Trisul. Loomis had an attack of cramp, but when he had recovered we turned our attention to the rock tower at our backs, on top of which we hoped to find better things. Lloyd did a grand lead up a steep rock chimney with his load on and was able to give the rest of us some much needed moral and, in my case, physical

A rest near the foot of the gully, *circa* 22,500 ft.

encouragement with the rope. This took some time and it was four
o'clock before we were all on top of the tower, where there was barely
room for five of us to stand, much less pitch a tent. Looking up the
ridge, it was impossible to say where such a place would be found, but
it was sufficiently broken to offer considerable hope. Meantime three
of us had to get back to Camp IV and at this time of the afternoon of
a bright sunny day the snow would be at its worst. With the assent of
all, it was decided to dump our loads here leaving Houston and Odell
to shift for themselves. It seemed a selfish decision at the time and it
seems so now; no doubt we could have cut it a bit finer and yet got
down before dark, but it was likely that they would not have to go
far before finding a bivouac, and, in any case, with sleeping bags and
warm clothing they could not come to much harm.

We learnt afterwards that they had an uncommonly busy evening.
They had to climb another 150 ft. before even the most imaginative
could discern the makings of a platform, and then they had to make
two journeys up and down with the loads. It was dark before they were
finally settled.

Oblivious of this activity and the curses which were being
bestowed, rather unjustly, on us for our premature desertion, we
climbed hastily but cautiously down, reaching the camp at sundown.
There was no sign of Graham Brown and Carter, so we assumed they
were having a day off at Camp III.

Discussing the results of this day's work, we decided the bivouac
was about 23,500 ft., probably too low for an attempt on the summit,
but as high as we could push it in the day. We thought they would
probably move it higher to-morrow and make their bid on the following day. The closer view of the upper part of the mountain which
we had obtained had not made it look any easier, and it was a puzzle
to make out where exactly the peak lay. I began to fear we had not
allowed them enough time, but now it was too late to alter plans.

Next day was fine, but mist shrouded the upper mountain from
our anxious gaze. We felt slack, and took the morning off before going
down to Camp III to give Graham Brown and Carter a hand with their
loads. As their tent was the one which had been half-buried by the blizzard, it took them a long time to dig it out, so we returned before them
and prepared a platform.

Circa 23,000 ft., the shallow gully—eastern Basin rim on right

The 27th was to be for us at Camp IV another day of idleness. That at least was the plan, but the event was different, and for some of us it was a day of the greatest mental and physical stress that we had yet encountered.

I had been worrying all night over the waste of this day, trying to devise some scheme whereby the second pair could go up at once to the bivouac. The trouble was that a second tent was essential, and having seen something of the extraordinary difficulty of finding a site even for the small tent, to go up there on the slim chance of finding a site for the big one as well was incurring the risk of exhausting the party to no purpose. While we were having breakfast, debating this knotty point and wondering how far the summit party had got, Loomis disclosed the fact that all was not well with his feet, the toes being slightly frostbitten, and that henceforward we should have to count him out. This loss of carrying power knocked the scheme for a second tent on the head and a few moments later we had something else to think about.

We had just decided they must be well on the way to the top when we were startled to hear Odell's familiar yodel, rather like the braying of an ass. It sounded so close that I thought they must be on the way down, having got the peak the previous day, but it suddenly dawned on us that he was trying to send an S.O.S. Carter, who had the loudest voice, went outside to try and open communication, and a few minutes later came back to the tent to announce that 'Charlie is killed'— Charlie being Houston. It was impossible to see anyone on the mountain, but he was certain he had heard correctly. As soon as we had pulled ourselves together, I stuffed some clothes and a bandage into a rucksack and Lloyd and I started off as fast as we could manage, to be followed later by Graham Brown and Carter with a hypodermic syringe.

It was a climb not easily forgotten—trying to go fast and realising that at this height it was impossible to hurry, wondering what we should find, and above all what we could do. The natural assumption was that there had been a fall, and that since they were sure to be roped, Odell was also hurt, and the chance of getting a helpless man down the mountain was too remote to bear thinking about. As if to confirm this assumption, we could get no answer to repeated calls on the way up.

Remembering our struggles yesterday on the ridge and in the chimney, we took a different line and tackled a band of steep rock directly above us, in between the gully and the ridge. It proved to be much worse than it looked and, when we had hauled ourselves panting on to the snow above, we vowed that the next time we would stick to the gully, which here narrowed and passed through a sort of cleft in the rock band.

The time was now about two o'clock, and traversing up and to the right over snow in the direction of the ridge, the little tent came in sight not thirty yards away. Instinctively we tried almost to break into a run, but it was no use, and we advanced step by step, at a maddening pace, not knowing what we should find in the tent, if indeed anything at all. The sight of an ice-axe was a tremendous relief; evidently Odell had managed to crawl back. But when another was seen, conjecture was at a loss. Then voices were heard talking quietly and next moment we were greeted with, 'Hullo, you blokes, have some tea.' 'Charlie is ill' was the message Odell had tried to convey!

Lloyd and I experienced a curious gamut of emotions; firstly and naturally, of profound relief, then, and I think not unnaturally, disgust at having suffered such unnecessary mental torture, and, of course, deep concern for Houston. While we swallowed tea, tea that reeked of pemmican but which I still remember with thankfulness, we heard what they had done and discussed what we were to do.

They had devoted yesterday to a reconnaissance. Following the ridge up they found, at a height of about 500 ft. above the bivouac, a flat snow platform capable of holding two tents comfortably. Beyond that the climbing became interesting and difficult, but they had reached the foot of a long and easy snow slope leading up to the final rock wall. Here they turned back, having decided to move the bivouac next day to the higher site. Both were going strongly, but early that night Houston became violently ill, and in the cramped quarters of the tent, perched insecurely on an inadequate platform above a steep slope, both had spent a sleepless and miserable night. Houston attributed his trouble to the bully beef which both had eaten; Odell was unaffected, but it is possible that a small portion was tainted and certainly the symptoms pointed to poisoning of some kind.

Houston was still very ill and very weak, but it was he who suggested what should be done, and showed us how evil might be turned to good. It was only possible for two people to stay up here, and his plan was that he should go down that afternoon and that I should stay up with Odell, and thus no time would have been lost. We demurred to this on the ground that he was not fit to move, but he was so insistent on the importance of not losing a day and so confident of being able to get down that we at last consented.

We all four roped up, with Houston in the middle, and started slowly down, taking frequent rests. We struck half-right across the snow and joined the gully above the rock band according to our earlier resolution, and there the two rear men anchored the party while Lloyd cut steps down the narrow cleft, which was very icy. Houston was steady enough in spite of his helpless state of weakness, and having safely negotiated this awkward bit, we kicked slowly down to the left and found our up-going tracks. Presently Graham Brown and Carter hove in sight, and I imagine their amazement at seeing four people coming down was as great as ours had been at the sight of the two ice-axes. When we met, Lloyd and Houston tied on to their rope and continued the descent, while Odell and I climbed slowly back to the bivouac.

This illness of Houston's was a miserable turn of fortune for him, robbing him as it did of the summit. Bad as he was, his generous determination to go down was of a piece with the rest of his actions.

CHAPTER XVI

THE TOP

———◆———

S CENICALLY THE POSITION of the bivouac was very fine but residen-
tially it was damnable. It was backed on two sides by rock, but on
the others the snow slope fell away steeply, and the platform which had
been scraped out in the snow was so narrow that the outer edge of the
tent overhung for almost a foot, thus reducing considerably both the
living space and any feeling one yet had of security. Necessity makes a
man bold, and I concluded that necessity had pressed very hard that
night when they lit on this spot for their bivouac. Odell, who had had
no sleep the previous night, could have slept on a church spire, and, as
I had Houston's sleeping bag and the extra clothing I had fortunately
brought up, we both had a fair night. Odell, who was the oldest inhab-
itant and in the position of host, generously conceded to me the outer
berth, overhanging space.

The weather on the 28th still held and without regret we packed
up our belongings and made the first trip to the upper bivouac. The
snow slope was steeper than any we had yet met but, at the early hour
we started, the snow was good and in an hour we reached the spacious
snow shelf which they had marked down. It was about 20 ft. x 20 ft., so
that there was room to move about, but on either side of the ridge on
which it stood the slope was precipitous. After a brief rest the increasing heat of the sun warned us to be on the move again and we hurried
down for the remaining loads. The snow was softening rapidly under
a hot sun nor was this deterioration confined only to the snow. We
already knew, and it was to be impressed on us again, that at these altitudes a hot sun is a handicap not to be lightly assessed.

Guessing the height of this camp, aided by the absence of the hypsometer, we put it at about 24,000 ft. Trisul was well below us and
even the top of East Nanda Devi (24,379 ft.) began to look less remote.
The condition of the wide belt of snow which had to be crossed, the difficulties of the final wall, and the weather were so many large question

marks, but we turned in that night full of hope, and determined to give ourselves every chance by an early start.

We were up at five o'clock to begin the grim business of cooking and the more revolting tasks of eating breakfast and getting dressed. That we were up is an exaggeration, we were merely awake, for all these fatigues are carried out from inside one's sleeping bag until it is no longer possible to defer the putting on of boots. One advantage a narrow tent has, that at lower altitudes is overlooked, is that the two sleeping bags are in such close proximity that boots which are rammed into the non-existent space between them generally survive the night without being frozen stiff. It worked admirably on this occasion so that we were spared the pangs of wrestling with frozen boots with cold fingers. Frozen boots are a serious matter and may cause much delay, and in order to mitigate this trouble we had, since the start, carefully refrained from oiling our boots. This notion might work well enough on Everest in pre-monsoon conditions where the snow is dry, but we fell between two stools, rejoicing in wet feet down below and frozen boots higher up.

By six o'clock we were ready, and shortly after we crawled outside, roped up, and started. It was bitterly cold, for the sun had not yet risen over the shoulder of East Nanda Devi and there was a thin wind from the west. What mugs we were to be fooling about on this infernal ridge at that hour of the morning! And what was the use of this ridiculous coil of rope, as stiff as a wire hawser, tying me for better or for worse to that dirty-looking ruffian in front! Such, in truth, were the reflections of at least one of us as we topped a snow boss behind the tent, and the tenuous nature of the ridge in front became glaringly obvious in the chill light of dawn. It was comforting to reflect that my companion in misery had already passed this way, and presently as the demands of the climbing became more insistent, grievances seemed less real, and that life was still worth living was a proposition that might conceivably be entertained.

This difficult ridge was about three hundred yards long, and though the general angle appeared slight it rose in a series of abrupt rock and snow steps. On the left was an almost vertical descent to a big ravine, bounded on the far side by terrific grey cliffs that supported the broad snow shelf for which we were making. The right side also fell

The first bivouac, 23,500 ft.

The second bivouac, 24,000 ft.

away steeply, being part of the great rock cirque running round to East Nanda Devi. The narrow ridge we were on formed a sort of causeway between the lower south face and the upper snow shelf.

One very important factor which, more than anything, tended to promote a happier frame of mind was that the soft crumbly rock had at last yielded to a hard rough schistose-quartzite which was a joy to handle; a change which could not fail to please us as mountaineers and, no doubt, to interest my companion as a geologist. That vile rock, schist is, I believe, the technical term, had endangered our heads and failed to support our feet from the foot of the scree to the last bivouac. It was a wonder our burning anathemas had not caused it to undergo a geological change under our very eyes—metamorphosed it, say, into plutonic rocks. But, as has been said by others, there is good in everything, and, on reflection, this very sameness was not without some saving grace because it meant that we were spared an accumulation of rock samples at every camp. A bag of assorted stones had already been left at the Glacier Camp, and I tremble to think what burdens we might have had to carry down the mountain had the rock been as variegated as our geologist, and indeed any right-minded geologist, would naturally desire.

Thanks to the earlier reconnaissance by him and Houston, Odell led over this ridge at a good pace and in an hour and a half we had reached the snow mound which marked the farthest point they had reached. It was a ridge on which we moved one at a time.

In front was a snow slope set at an angle of about 30 degrees and running right up to the foot of the rock wall, perhaps 600 or 700 ft. above us. To the west this wide snow terrace extended for nearly a quarter of a mile until it ended beneath that same skyline ridge, which below had formed the western boundary of the broad gully. On our right the shelf quickly steepened and merged into the steep rock face of the ridge between East Nanda Devi and our mountain. We were too close under the summit to see where it lay, but there was little doubt about the line we should take, because from a rapid survey there seemed to be only one place where a lodgement could be effected on the final wall. This was well to the west of our present position, where a snow rib crossed the terrace at right angles and, abutting against the wall, formed as it were a ramp.

We began the long snow trudge at eight o'clock and even at that early hour and after a cold night the snow was not good and soon became execrable. The sun was now well up. After it had been at work for a bit we were going in over our knees at every step, and in places where the slope was steeper it was not easy to make any upward progress at all. One foot would be lifted and driven hard into the snow and then, on attempting to rise on it, one simply sank down through the snow to the previous level. It was like trying to climb up cotton wool, and a good deal more exhausting, I imagine, than the treadmill. But, like the man on a walking tour in Ireland, who throughout a long day received the same reply of '20 miles' to his repeated inquiries as to the distance he was from his destination, we could at any rate say, 'Thank God, we were holding our own.'

The exertion was great and every step made good cost six to eight deep breaths. Our hopes of the summit grew faint, but there was no way but to plug on and see how far we could get. This we did, thinking only of the next step, taking our time, and resting frequently. It was at least some comfort that the track we were ploughing might assist a second party. On top of the hard work and the effect of altitude was the languor induced by a sun which beat down relentlessly on the dazzling snow, searing our lips and sapping the energy of mind and body. As an example of how far this mind-sapping process had gone, I need only mention that it was seriously suggested that we should seek the shade of a convenient rock which we were then near, lie up there until evening, and finish the climb in the dark!

It is noteworthy that whilst we were enjoying, or more correctly enduring, this remarkable spell of sunshine, the foothills south and west of the Basin experienced disastrous floods. As related in the first chapter, it was on this day that the Pindar river overflowed sweeping away some houses in the village of Tharali, while on the same day nineteen inches of rain fell at the hill station of Mussoorie west of Ranikhet.

We derived some encouragement from seeing East Nanda Devi sink below us and at one o'clock, rather to our surprise, we found ourselves on top of the snow rib moving at a snail's pace towards the foot of the rocks. There we had a long rest and tried to force some chocolate down our parched throats by eating snow at the same time. Though neither of us said so, I think both felt that now it would take a lot to stop us. There was a difficult piece of rock to climb; Odell led this and appeared to find it stimulating, but it provoked me to exclaim loudly upon its 'thinness'. Once over that, we were landed fairly on the final slope with the summit ridge a bare 300 ft. above us.

Presently we were confronted with the choice of a short but very steep snow gully and a longer but less drastic route to the left. We took the first and found the snow reasonably hard owing to the very steep angle at which it lay. After a severe struggle I drew myself out of it on to a long and gently sloping corridor, just below and parallel to the summit ridge. I sat down and drove the axe in deep to hold Odell as he finished the gully. He moved up to join me and I had just suggested the corridor as a promising line to take when there was a sudden hiss and, quicker than thought, a slab of snow, about forty yards long, slid off the corridor and disappeared down the gully, peeling off a foot of snow as it went. At the lower limit of the avalanche, which was where we were sitting, it actually broke away for a depth of a foot all round my axe to which I was holding. At its upper limit, forty yards up the corridor, it broke away to a depth of three or four feet.

The corridor route had somehow lost its attractiveness, so we finished the climb by the ridge without further adventure, reaching the top at three o'clock.

The summit is not the exiguous and precarious spot that usually graces the top of so many Himalayan peaks, but a solid snow ridge nearly two hundred yards long and twenty yards broad. It is seldom that conditions on top of a high peak allow the climber the time or the opportunity to savour the immediate fruits of victory.

Too often, when having first carefully probed the snow to make sure he is not standing on a cornice, the climber straightens up preparatory to savouring the situation to the full, he is met by a perishing wind and the interesting view of a cloud at close quarters, and with a muttered imprecation turns in his tracks and begins the descent. Far otherwise was it now. There were no cornices to worry about and room to unrope and walk about. The air was still, the sun shone, and the view was good if not so extensive as we had hoped.

Odell had brought a thermometer, and no doubt sighed for the hypsometer. From it we found that the air temperature was

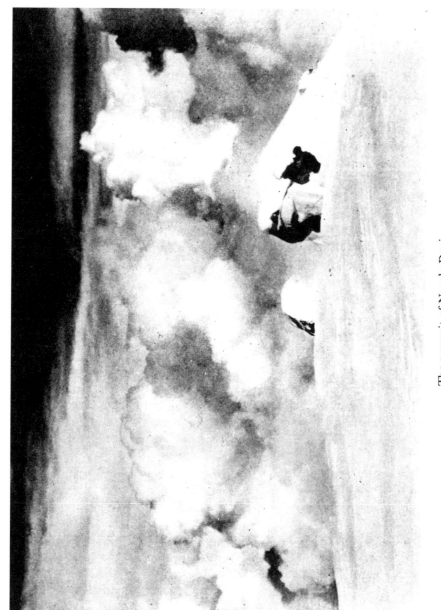

The summit of Nanda Devi

20 degrees F., but in the absence of wind we could bask gratefully in the friendly rays of our late enemy the sun. It was difficult to realise that we were actually standing on top of the same peak which we had viewed two months ago from Ranikhet, and which had then appeared incredibly remote and inaccessible, and it gave us a curious feeling of exaltation to know that we were above every peak within hundreds of miles on either hand. Dhaulagiri, 1000 ft. higher, and two hundred miles away in Nepal, was our nearest rival. I believe we so far forgot ourselves as to shake hands on it.

After the first joy in victory came a feeling of sadness that the mountain had succumbed, that the proud head of the goddess was bowed.

At this late hour of the day there was too much cloud about for any distant views. The Nepal peaks were hidden and all the peaks on the rim, excepting only Trisul, whose majesty even our loftier view-point could not diminish. Far to the north through a vista of white cloud the sun was colouring to a warm brown the bare and bleak Tibetan plateau.

After three-quarters of an hour on that superb summit, a brief forty-five minutes into which was crowded the worth of many hours of glorious life, we dragged ourselves reluctantly away, taking with us a memory that can never fade and leaving behind 'thoughts beyond the reaches of our souls'.

If our thoughts were still treading on air, the short steep gully, swept by the avalanche bare of steps, soon brought us to earth. We kicked slowly down it, facing inwards and plunging an arm deep into the snow for support. Followed another exhausting drag across the snow, hindered rather than helped by the deep holes we had made coming up, and then a cold hour was spent moving cautiously, one at a time, down the ice and the benumbing rocks of the long ridge above the bivouac. We paused to watch a bird, a snow pigeon, cross our ridge and fly swiftly across the grey cliffs of the ravine beneath the snow ter-race, like the spirit of Nanda Devi herself, forsaking the fastness which was no longer her own.

At six o'clock we reached the tent and brewed the first of many jorums of tea. After such a day nothing could have tasted better and our appreciation was enhanced by our long enforced abstinence. There

Cliffs on left of route above Camp VI, Rishi gorge below

was but a pinch left and we squandered it all recklessly, saving the leaves for the morning. Food was not even mentioned.

We paid for this debauch with a sleepless night to which no doubt exhaustion and a still-excited imagination contributed. Each little incident of the climb was gone over again and again, and I remember, in the small hours when the spark of life burns lowest, the feeling which predominated over all was one of remorse at the fall of a giant. It is the same sort of contrition that one feels at the shooting of an elephant, for however thrilling and arduous the chase, however great has been the call upon skill, perseverance, and endurance, and however gratifying the weight of the ivory, when the great bulk crashes to the ground achievement seems to have been bought at the too high cost of sacrilege.

It was very cold next morning when we packed up and started down. Near the bottom of the gully we were met by Lloyd and Loomis, who were coming up to help us down and who were overjoyed when they heard that success had crowned the efforts of the whole party. Houston and Graham Brown had already gone down and we decided to stop the night at Camp IV. There were still three or four days' food left in hand but Loomis and Carter were both troubled with their feet, which must have been touched with frost the day Camp IV was occupied. Lloyd was going stronger than ever and it was much to be regretted that we could not make up a second party.

The weather, which during this crucial period had been so kind, now broke up and on the morning of the 31st it was blowing half a gale out of a clear sky. Lloyd, Loomis, and I started some time before the other two, all carrying heavy loads because we left nothing but the two big tents, some snow-shoes, and two pairs of crampons or ice-claws. The snow-shoes had been lugged up to assist us on soft snow and the crampons for use on hard snow, but the slopes were, of course, all too steep for snow-shoes, and the only time we might have used the crampons was now when they had been abandoned.

It was bitterly cold, and the snow on the arête was hard and dangerous—the mountain had not finished with us yet. We started to descend in the usual way, plunging the heel in at each step with a stiff leg. When one or two 'voluntaries' had been cut, we should have taken warning that the snow was not right for such tactics, but we were all pretty tired and in a hurry to get down, and it is in such circumstances that care is relaxed and the party comes to grief. Fortunately before this happened we had another warning which could not well be ignored. The leader's heels went from under him and he slid down the slope pulling the second man after him until checked by the rope belayed round the end man's axe, which fortunately held firm. We all felt rather ashamed of ourselves after this exhibition and abandoned that method in favour of the slower but safer one of cutting steps and moving one at a time, which should have been adopted at the start.

There was another slip, quickly checked, when one of the snow steps above the Gîte gave way, and we reached this camp in a chastened frame of mind and hoping that the mountain had now exhausted its spite. After a brief rest we pushed on, unroped gladly when we were off the snow, and picked our way with great caution down the unstable rocks to Camp I. On the way we noticed with concern that Odell and Carter were still high up on the arête and moving very slowly.

We found here Graham Brown and Pasang. The former's leg was troubling him, so he had spent the night here where there were still two tents, and Pasang had come up from below to take his load. We heard that Graham Brown and Houston too had narrowly escaped disaster on the previous day by the breaking of a step above the Gîte. Pasang had completely recovered his sight, but he was not yet his former bright self, for I think he felt keenly the disability which prevented him from helping his Sahibs at grips with the mountain.

It was now midday and after a drink of cocoa, which served only to bring home to us the loss we had suffered, we continued the descent. The cocoa so wrought upon Lloyd that, with a desperation born of thirst, he turned aside to prosecute a last and unsuccessful search for the tea. On the Coxcomb ridge I met Phuta going up to help Pasang and was shocked to hear that Kitar had died in the night. We got down to the new Base Camp at the foot of the scree at two o'clock and but for the melancholy news of Kitar's death there was nothing to mar our contentment. Twenty-one days had elapsed since we left.

CHAPTER XVII

A NEW PASS

H OUSTON HAD ALMOST RECOVERED, Da Namgyal was there, still coughing, but obviously bursting to lay out Odell's pyjamas. He had brought with him six men from Lata, the mail, and one or two luxuries which had been scrapped at the Bridge Camp. Best of all, one of our old Mana men had come with them bringing a letter of greeting and a present from the Rawal of Badrinath—an enormous basket of apples, nuts, potatoes, and other vegetables, than which nothing, not excepting a tin of tea, could have been more acceptable. After living as we had been, any fresh food is the greatest luxury imaginable; many of our idle hours had been passed in devising the sort of meal for which each of us most longed, and in every imaginary menu fruit bulked large. We were deeply touched by this kindly and thoughtful act on the part of one who had already helped us in every way he could. Fortunately some of the party were able to visit Badrinath on the way back and thank our benefactor personally.

Not the least of our delights was that of being, if not on grass, at any rate on the sort of soil which looked as if, with very little encouragement, it might grow grass, and that did in fact support some moss and scant herbage. To our starved senses it looked like an oasis and smelt divinely. Fresh water to drink in unstinted measure, a wood fire to look at, bare feet on warm earth, the cry of a marmot, such were the simple things which now gave us unbounded pleasure. Some averred that the air felt and tasted differently, and on the mountain they went so far as to claim that this difference could be felt on going down from Camp III to Camp II; but speaking personally, provided of course one sits still, I would not undertake to say whether the air I was breathing was that of 10,000 ft. or 20,000 ft.

While we were on the mountain Emmons had not been idle, having almost completed a plane-table survey of the South-East glacier and its tributaries. He had further made a valiant and almost successful attempt to reach the top of 'Longstaff's Col', accompanied only by the inexperienced Kalu. Kalu apparently had worked very well and was once more in the mood for chest-beating. In the midst of these activities he, Emmons, had had two sick men to look after, Kitar and Nuri. Kitar got steadily worse in spite of all that could be done for him in the way of medicines and special food, and on the night of the 30th he died. He was buried before we got down, and on his grave the Sherpas built a large cairn and fenced it about with a ring of stones. He sleeps amongst the mountains to which he had given of his best, to which his long record of service is eloquent testimony. He had probably served on more major expeditions than any other Sherpa living. Nuri was still with us, but more wasted and woebegone than ever, and so weak as to cause us some anxiety. The other porters had recovered, Pasang his sight and Nima his cheery grin.

By evening it was snowing hard, but that did not prevent Emmons and Houston from preparing for us, and serving, a supper that put to shame any previous efforts. Odell and Carter had not yet arrived but, knowing our geologist by now, we were not unduly worried and thought they might be spending the night at Camp I. However, as darkness fell they came down the scree, soaked to the skin and dog-tired. It was too late now for the mountain to strike back.

September 1st was a day of luxurious idleness devoted to settling plans for our return. I was bent on attempting to force a new route out of the Basin by 'Longstaff's Col' and Houston was keen to come too, despite the fact that it was imperative for him to be in Ranikhet by the 13th, and no one could tell how long it would take us. Of the others, all were anxious to see Badrinath of which they had heard so much, and Emmons wanted another day or two in the Basin to complete his survey.

On the 2nd the various caravans got under way; first to leave was Nuri, carrying no load, for in his feeble state he wanted a long start. He was followed by Graham Brown, Lloyd, and Odell, with a most ambitious programme which entailed double-marching all the way— we called them the 'express'. Then Loomis and Carter pushed off with most of the porters carrying the surplus gear—they were the 'slow freight'. Emmons and Kalu then departed, bound for the other side of the glacier, after a moving display of chest-thumping by Kalu. If he got safely across the glacier he would have something to thump about, for his load was of staggering dimensions. Finally Houston, Pasang, and I left about midday in a snow storm, travelling as light as possible and bound for a bivouac at the foot of the snow slope below the Pass.

The 'express' and the 'slow freight' seem to have changed roles soon after starting, the 'express' having trouble with its feet. Ranikhet was reached in the reverse order to that of leaving the Basin, and some time behind schedule.

We three followed up the true right bank of the glacier and crossed it when it began to curve round at the foot of the Coxcomb ridge. We were armed with a plan, drawn by Emmons, showing us where he had made his bivouac, but we misled ourselves by assuming his progress was as slow as our own and, failing to find it, camped on snow, all in one tent, some way below it. The height was about 17,500 ft., the col is 19,200 ft., so we made preparations for a very early start. We took a gloomy view of our chances of getting over on account of the snow which had fallen that day and was still falling that night.

We were up at 3.30 a.m. and left at five on a fine morning, creeping along at the foot of a rock wall. The snow was soft, filling us with alarm and despondency, but once we were clear of the rocks it hardened up and soon we had to scrape out steps with our ice-axes. The slope steepened rapidly and we made for an outcrop of rock over to our right, where we thought we would be more comfortable and which would, when scaled, lead us to the foot of a snow rib set at a slightly easier angle than the rest of the face. We had studied the approach to this col long and earnestly from our camps on the mountain in all conditions of light and shadow; always hoping for, but never receiving, some slight hint that it was not really as steep as it looked. Coming up last night we had caught a distorted glimpse of it through snow and swirling mists, when it looked ridiculously easy, but now, as every step brought us closer under it, our first impressions were not only confirmed but deepened.

After tentative essays to effect a lodgement on the rock bulge in two different places, we decided there was too much verglas on the rock for safety, and retreated stealthily to the snow. We climbed up till level with the top of the rocks and then began traversing across above the outcrop in order to gain the snow rib. The snow of the traverse was horribly deep and loose and, with no supporting snow below but only rock, conditions seemed ideal for an avalanche. It was with considerable misgiving that we crept slowly and cautiously across it, but the rib was temptingly close and the alternative route straight up the snow to our left was minatory in its steepness. The sun, which was now well over the wall above us, added to our anxiety, but the snow held, and once astride, literally astride, the rib we breathed more freely. For the first few feet of this the snow was rather worse than that which we had experienced near the top of Nanda Devi, and for every step up we sank down two. After tremendous exertions we struggled up a few feet and then began to find solid bottom. A prolonged bout of step-kicking landed us on top of the col at eleven o'clock.

For most of the way up the weather was clear and there was a magnificent view of our ridge on Nanda Devi seen in profile. I had brought a camera solely for the purpose of taking this invaluable picture, but it was stowed away in the bottom of my rucksack which was in turn part of a load, strapped to a carrying frame. Once we were fairly committed to the difficult part of the climb there was little inclination or opportunity for getting it out; but that is a feeble excuse and with a little trouble the thing could have been done—but I kept on putting off the evil moment. Now, of course, when we sat down exhausted on the top of the pass the whole mountain had disappeared in the mist. Had we been higher I might cite this as a fair sample of high-altitude mentality, but since we were only 19,000 ft. the less said about it the better. One lesson at least it teaches, which is not to carry your camera in a rucksack, and the corollary to that is a small, light camera.

Our field of view was restricted to within a hundred yards of where we sat, but we had looked at the pass and its neighbourhood so long and frequently that we knew, or thought we knew, the topography of it. We were on the eastern rim of the Basin at the foot of the long shoulder which runs up to East Nanda Devi. To the south the rim climbs for a thousand feet to form the fluted ice wall which towers above the main arm of the South-East glacier. From somewhere on this ice wall and outside the Basin, a ridge extends eastwards linking Nanda Kot with the Nanda Devi group. On this ridge, between the Sanctuary wall and Nanda Kot, there is a pass, called Traill's Pass after the first Commissioner of Kumaon, whose administration lasted from 1815 to 1835. He was also the first to cross this pass in 1830, and it has been suggested that his object was not mountain exploration but to find a short cut between the Pindar valley and Milam which would be useful for commercial purposes. The pass is 17,700 ft. high, and whatever his object it was a very remarkable feat for one who was not a mountaineer and who lived almost before the dawn of mountaineering. Since then it has been crossed in 1855 by Adolph Schlagintweit as related in chapter 1, in 1861 by Colonel Edmund Smyth, and again in 1926 by a party which included Mr Hugh Ruttledge. The Pass leads to the Pindari glacier and from there to Ranikhet is a short and easy route, so it was attractive to us for that reason as well as for the few times which it had been crossed.

On the east side of the col, or what might now truly be called the Pass, a slope of rock and snow, decidedly less steep than the Basin side, led down to the Milam valley. This was a known and suitable route for us to take, but we had not yet given up hope of finding and crossing Traill's Pass, although the heavy mist was a severe handicap. Our very distant surveys from high on Nanda Devi had led us to think that the ridge on which the Pass lay was not far from where we now sat, and we thought that by traversing to our right we might arrive somewhere in the vicinity of the Pass without losing much height—a consideration which in our then feeble state of mind and body seemed of paramount importance. We sat there for an hour waiting for a clearing in which we might see something of what lay between us and the Pass. No clearing came, so we began traversing blindly.

After we had been going for two hours on steep, soft, and rather unsafe snow, the mist was as thick as ever and we appeared to be getting nowhere except, possibly, into trouble. We gave up traversing and began casting about for a tent site, and in the process we were driven lower and lower down the slope. When there was still no sign of a suitable platform and it was getting late, we decided to go straight down to the glacier, although we knew that this probably meant the abandonment of Traill's Pass. We were all very tired and made a sorry job of the descent, getting into trouble in a long ice runnel which was like a water-course full of ice. I was in front of the others and, after one or two involuntary glissades, had half made up my mind to forsake the firm but dangerous going in the icy channel for the safe but laborious snow-plodding on the bank above. My mind was made up for me by

'Longstaff's Col' (19,200) and Nanda Kot (22,500 ft.)

a boulder which came spinning down and which I only just managed to dodge. With more haste than dignity I scrambled up the bank. We finally camped at about half-past five on what was almost a grass sward a few hundred feet above the Lwanl glacier. For once Pasang seemed to have had enough.

Talking things over that night we reluctantly gave up an attempt on the Pass and decided to go home via the Milam valley. Having lost so much height we were not in the right trim for facing a climb up again and, though the valley route might be longer, in the weather and snow conditions prevailing it was conceivable that once more the longest way round might be the shortest way home.

Next morning, lightened by the scrapping of the Primus stove and some paraffin, we descended to the glacier, crossed it to the north side and followed it down to below the snout. There was the usual stream, here only in its infancy, issuing from the glacier, but, mindful of the ways of these streams, I decided that we would do well to get on the Ranikhet side of it while we could. I therefore forded it without much difficulty, but Pasang, seeing a likely looking line of country ahead and sniffing the fleshpots from afar, went off at score down the north bank where Houston, for his sins, followed him. Walking along our respective banks of the river we came soon to the grazing alp of Narspati which lies under the northern slopes of Nanda Kot. Looking back, the whole head of the valley was filled with the magnificent bulk of East Nanda Devi, seen with advantage from a fresh angle and no longer overshadowed by its namesake, which was now hidden away behind it. West of the glistening pile of Nanda Kot, with its familiar tabletop, was the long low ridge which we should then have been crossing by Traill's Pass. It was much farther away from our pass than we had imagined nor did the Pass look by any means a walk-over.

There were here a few stone huts on both sides of the river, but on the north side there was also a well-marked path, along which I watched Pasang disappearing with envy. On my side the river lapped the foot of the moraine of a big glacier coming down from Nanda Kot, and soon I was blaspheming and boulder-hopping along this in a very evil frame of mind. Presently the going became so bad that I decided to climb 200 ft. up to the top of the moraine, where I thought I would find better going or even the path, which I was convinced must exist from the evidence of the stone huts. But this exhausting climb was to no purpose, I had merely exchanged boulder-hopping on a slope for boulder-hopping on the razor-backed moraine top, and my already sour temper grew worse as I thought how the other two must be enjoying my antics from the security of their path.

Having won clear of the boulders of the glacier I did find a sort of path and, hurrying along to catch up, I at length saw the others waiting for me on the opposite bank. It was impossible to carry on any conversation above the roar of the river, which was now a formidable torrent, but they were complacent enough to suggest by signs that I should try to cross it, at which I shook my head with terrific violence and signalled a counter suggestion that it was time they joined me. Then I remembered that Houston was carrying all our chocolate and by pointing to my mouth I got him to throw some over. We lunched amicably but distantly and then pursued our divided but parallel courses.

I could see what was happening on their steeply sloping bank much better than they could and, while my path steadily improved, I could see that there was trouble ahead for them in a series of big landslides, which could only be circumvented by using another path much higher up. They failed to spot this path and presently got spread-eagled on the almost vertical earth cliff left by the landslide. I gesticulated wildly to indicate that they must go up, but they seemed to think I was merely 'registering' enjoyment of their discomfiture, as perhaps I was, and paid no attention.

Finding themselves at last completely baffled they climbed wearily up and found the track, and we all started legging it for Martoli, the first village and the place where our respective paths would, in the fullness of time, unite. More trouble of the same sort awaited them round the next bend and, seeing this, I pushed on, leaving them to it, bent on vindicating my judgment by arriving before them, but never imagining it would be so thoroughly vindicated as it was.

While yet some three miles from Martoli and with no sign of my rivals on the other bank, I suddenly came upon a tributary river, and was dismayed to find the path turning off at right angles to follow up this side valley for one and a half miles, where it crossed the river by a bridge and then came back down the other side for a like distance, before once more following the main valley down to Martoli.

This extra three miles was an unexpected blow for I imagined that they would soon be gloating over my receding back as I toiled up this side valley, getting farther from Martoli every minute. However, there was no help, though all was not yet lost and, putting on all steam, an hour and a half later I was back in the main valley, very much hotter in mind and body and scanning the opposite slopes eagerly for signs of my pursuers. There was nothing to be seen and it seemed hardly possible that they could be already out of sight ahead. I noticed that as it approached Martoli the opposing slope grew steeper and steeper, and below the village, which was perched high up on my side, the river flowed through a deep gorge—nor was there a bridge nor any sign of a path leading to a bridge.

Reflecting that this would give them something to think about, I pushed on and reached Martoli at three o'clock.

CHAPTER XVIII

THE BHOTIAS OF MARTOLI

◆

Martoli is on one of the main trade routes between India and Tibet and is the last village but one (which is Milam) on the Indian side of the border. Situated on a high spur between the Gori and Lwanl rivers, 11,000 ft. up, it is a bleak and desolate spot, surrounded by high hills and swept by piercing winds. It is occupied by a population of about two hundred Bhotias. 'Occupied' is the word rather than inhabited, because these people only come up here in the early summer with their sheep, and go down again in October to pass the winter at Munsiara and other villages lower down the Gori valley. All food has to be brought up, for nothing is grown there except a little mustard and potatoes; but the grazing is excellent, and juniper and rhododendron bushes supply fuel. The houses are solidly built of stone and roofed with heavy slate, and are usually in the form of a hollow square surrounding a flagged courtyard.

About these most interesting people, the Bhotias, and their trade with Tibet, much could be written, but I must attempt only a brief sketch. As has been said, the Bhotias are of Mongolian extraction and speak a dialect akin to Tibetan. Bhot or Bod is really the same word as Tibet, but the people of Garhwal and Almora seldom use either of these names when referring to the country north of them, but call it Hundes. They have been Hinduised to a certain extent and worship not only Tibetan deities but also the gods of the Hindu pantheon. But they are not very orthodox Hindus, and the caste system is interpreted as it suits them. In the matter of food they are quite ready to eat with Tibetans, which would be defilement to strict Hindus, but which is probably of advantage to the Bhotias in their trade relations; nor did the Garhwal Bhotias show much scruple about eating any of our foods. Of their character it can be said that they are cheerful, hardy, industrious (at least the women), honest, hospitable, charitable, and a thoroughly likeable people. Nor are they the wild uncivilised barbarians that is sometimes thought. Their houses are well built and have some pretence to architecture; they are shrewd traders, willing to be educated, and have produced such men as Rai Kishen Singh Bahadur, the famous Pandit 'A.K.' of the Indian Survey, and one or two others who have earned a name for themselves in the exploration and mapping of Tibet.

The Bhotias enjoy a monopoly of the trade with Tibet, which appears to be a lucrative one in spite of the many taxes imposed by the Tibetans. The route from Milam to Tibet involves the crossing of three passes between 17,000 and 18,000 ft., all of which have to be crossed in one day because there is no grazing in between. The two chief markets to which the Bhotias of this valley resort are Gyanema and Gartok. The latter is a journey of five days or ten when travelling with sheep. In the spring the local Tibetan official visits Milam and, having first assured himself that there is no epidemic disease in the Bhotia villages, he levies a general toll before declaring the passes open. Further taxes are paid in Tibet. At one time the Indian Government decreed that no taxes were to be paid to the Tibetans, but when the Tibetans replied by closing the passes, the Bhotias were so hard hit that at their request the decree was rescinded. Tibet produces very little grain and is largely dependent on imports from India; wheat, barley, rice, therefore, are the chief articles carried in by the Bhotias, but sugar, tobacco, brass, copper, and iron are also taken. In return they bring from Tibet wool, salt, borax, yaks' tails, ponies, and of these the wool is by far the most important. The figure of 400 tons of wool for the year 1907 is an impressive one when the route and the means of transport are considered. The Bhotia traders and their households come up to Milam and Martoli in the spring and establish depots there, and in the course of the summer they make two or three journeys into Tibet. In the early autumn they begin sending their wool, salt, and borax to centres in the southern valleys, and by early November Milam and Martoli are once more deserted. Goats and sheep are the principal carriers, but yaks, jibbus, and mules are sometimes used. No fodder is carried for these, and in consequence the greater part of each day must be devoted to grazing. Marches are therefore short, seldom exceeding six or seven miles.

There is romance in trade and not least in this carried on in the grim defiles and over the stern passes of the Himalaya.

And now to continue the story of our strange antics on this the first day of our return to the habitations of man. I sat down beneath a low stone wall in the middle of the village to avoid the wind and to await the event. A crowd soon began to gather, as it would in an English village if someone dropped out of the skies, and a barrage of questions was fired at me. Their own knowledge of the country to the west stopped at the grazing alp of Narspati; beyond was hearsay, and they found it difficult to believe that anyone could have come over the icy barrier which lies west of this; if I had flown there they could not have been more surprised. When I had got it into their heads that we had come from Joshimath, climbing Nanda Devi on the way, they were profoundly impressed and showed an insatiable curiosity about our experiences on the mountain. Time and again they asked me if we had seen the goddess on top of the mountain, and when I was obliged to confess that we had noticed nothing but snow they seemed loth to believe it, and returned to the charge with suggestions that we must at any rate have seen the house in which the goddess dwelt. My boots, ice-axe, rope, clothes, face, and beard were all appraised and commented upon, fortunately in a language which I could not understand, and having thus provided them with considerable free instruction, entertainment, and amusement, I thought it was their turn and hinted that a little food and drink would not come amiss. Enormous thick chapatties, some blistering hot curry, and Tibetan tea, were soon forthcoming, and the clumsy way I handled the curry with my fingers amply repaid the donor.

A wet mist now blew up the valley and the whole party adjourned to a low, stone, windowless building, and the noise inside made it unnecessary for them to tell me it was the village school. Fifty diminutive Bhotia infants, boys and girls, were turned out, and the schoolmaster with one or two favourite pupils did the honours. He was a man of the world, and to impress upon me that at least one man in Martoli was not an ignorant savage he sent over to his house for a Thermos flask, of all things. It was full of very hot Tibetan tea, flavoured with red pepper, and at the moment I could not have too much to drink. But before I was allowed to start every man in the crowd had to stick his fingers down the mouth of it, not to enhance the flavour of the tea, as of course it did, but to assure himself that there was no deception about this modern miracle. While I was drinking, the favourite pupils were put through their paces, the most advanced had to write a sentence in Hindustani (in Roman characters I was relieved to find), and to this I had to write a suitable reply which the unfortunate scholar had then to read aloud for the edification of the audience. He passed the examination with far more credit than I did.

I found these mental exercises rather exhausting and welcomed a diversion in the shape of some 'chang' which one of my well-wishers brought along. This is a thin whitish beer made from barley and no Tibetan is ever far away from it. Just as we were settling down happily to some solemnish drinking a cry went up outside and we all trooped out to investigate. The excitement was caused by the strange spectacle of two men clinging like flies to the cliffs on the far side of the gorge. At first I thought it must be two enthusiasts of the Martoli Mountaineering Club, if such there was, enjoying a little practice on the local crags, but soon, in the failing light, I realised that it was Houston and Pasang looking for some means of reaching the haven where they would be, and, at almost the same moment, that they were not at all likely to find it. I was told that the bridge was a mile below the gorge and that they were away off the path to it. I suggested that someone should go over and show them the way, but it was obvious that nothing would be done, for it was now almost dark—besides there was a lot of beer left. We returned to the school.

When the party broke up I was not allowed to take up quarters on the earth floor of the school as I hoped. Under the guidance of the schoolmaster we stumbled in the dark through narrow lanes between house walls, colliding several times with what seemed to be the town band, a gang of youths who paraded the village after sundown, singing and beating a sort of tattoo on drums. Presently we turned through a narrow tunnel and emerged in a large courtyard about thirty yards square, and, stumbling first over a yak and then over some goats, I was led up a stone staircase and into a little room which seemed to be a kind of store. There were bales of wool, sheepskins, skins of bharal and musk deer, baskets of grain, and a couple of hand-dressed mill stones. There was a primitive oil lamp and a carpet was spread on the floor, so I hung up my hat and took possession. Then the genial Bhotia who was my host arrived, bringing with him my supper of curry and

Dancing girl in Martoli village

Women weaving cloth

rice and a few intimate friends to watch me dispatch it. This done I distributed tobacco and one of them produced some fiery home-made brandy. It had been too hard a day for me to shine socially and, when I nearly fell asleep where I sat, they took the hint and withdrew.

My host insisted on sleeping in the store with me, rather, I hope and believe, to ensure that nobody stole anything from me than that I should appropriate anything of his. He spent half the night measuring out rations of flour to one of his drovers who was going on a journey next day, and he was up before four to see the sheep loaded with their saddle bags. This activity did not disturb me, for I was too tired, nor did the bales of wool, which I had remarked with concern, discharge the clouds of fleas that I expected.

I was out at daylight next morning to have a look round but was not earlier than the women, who had already settled down to their endless task of weaving, seated round the courtyard at their twelve-foot lengths of cloth in the making, darting the shuttle through, and pressing the woof home with flat wooden staves. The spinning of thread for the weaving is done by the men and the children, who are never without a hank of wool on one wrist, which they spin into thread on a wooden spindle, as naturally as breathing, and half-unconsciously like a woman knitting.

The village is, as I have said, on a high bluff in the angle between the main Gori river and the tributary Lwanl stream down which we had come. To the north the valley is open and grassy, and nine miles away is Milam, the last village on the road and a much more important one than Martoli. Walking out of the village that morning, towards the end of the spur, I could look down on to the bridge over the Lwanl 400 ft. below, and beyond it to the white ribbon of road leading up the valley to Milam, whose position was indicated by the shining Milam peak. Down this road and across the bridge came flock after flock of white sheep and goats, bringing their burdens of wool, salt, and borax, from distant Tibet. Some took the valley road below the village but many climbed the steep zigzag track up to Martoli, and as they gained the flat plateau on which the village stands they were met by the band of last night and escorted to their owner's house in triumph with tap of drum. The patient plodding yaks and the jostling sheep, many of them lame and all of them tired, seemed to take fresh heart; it was for all the world like a footsore regiment being played into billets after a long march.

There was no one to play the two weary, belated wanderers in. I spotted them on the far side of the river accompanied by a third man, evidently a guide. They came slowly up the hill, wading knee-deep amongst a sea of sheep, and when Pasang saw me sitting there, trying hard to suppress a malicious grin, he had the grace to look sheepish himself. Perhaps I have dwelt too long on this incident, but to me at the time it afforded more amusement than it may when set down on paper, because so often the boot is on the other leg—it is the Sherpa who hits off the best route and the Sahib who is the fool.

We all returned to my lodging, where we ate eggs and potatoes and Houston told of their adventures. They had left the track which they should have followed because it turned up the hill away from the river and the village, and they were further betrayed by the sight of a man coming down from Martoli towards the river, whom they rashly assumed to be making for a crossing place. By dusk they were deeply involved on the cliffs above the gorge where I had seen them, and when they had extricated themselves they had to go back up the valley for a good half mile before finding a camping place. In the morning they chanced upon a shepherd who took them to the bridge by a short cut.

While we were breakfasting a man, a girl, and a baby came into the courtyard, and while the man played on a drum with his hands, the baby being parked at his side, the girl danced and sang in a blood-curdling falsetto. She hardly moved off the flat stone on which she stood and expressed more with her hands and her body than with her feet. Occasionally she stopped to pass round the hat in the form of the shovel-shaped basket which is used for winnowing, but her performance impressed by its sustained effort more than by its beauty. However, it seemed to be appreciated by the weaving women, the idlers, and by a small party who, having slaughtered a sheep, were busy cutting it up alongside the man holding the drum and the baby. Nor did the sheep, goats, yaks, cows, and mules, sunning themselves on the warm stones of the courtyard, show any violent symptoms of dislike. Contributions of grain, rice, and bits of wool found their way into the basket and we, with mistaken generosity, added a four-anna piece. This was fatal, because the girl promptly took up a position close to Houston, who was foolishly sitting outside, and gyrated in front of him till he was dizzy and fled inside for refuge.

We did not want to leave the protection of our room until this dangerous dancing girl had gone, but she showed no signs of stopping and it was time to think of starting, although the hospitable Bhotias wanted us to stop and make another night of it. We tried to hire two porters to carry our loads, but no one would come for less than the outrageous rate of Rs 3 a day and, like the Mr Ramsbottom in the song 'Runcorn Ferry' who would 'sooner be drownded than done', we continued to carry our own packs. Then came the question of settling with the good people of Martoli for my board and lodging and the food we had bought, and in that I am afraid my host's trading instincts overcame his geniality; not in the amount asked, for that was only Rs 3, but in a little comedy that was acted for our benefit. Having nothing else, we tendered a five-rupee note, and after a prolonged absence our host returned with the sad news that there was no change in the village. We offered him a 120 ft. climbing rope in full settlement, but as this would not do we took back the five rupee note. That worried him a lot and off he went again to return at last with one rupee. We were hard-hearted enough to refuse this, and the whole farce was re-enacted and that time one and a half rupees were forthcoming. It was a consummate piece of acting, but by now we had tumbled to it, so, pocketing our five rupees, we shouldered our packs, said goodbye and walked off, when of course he at once produced, quite unabashed, the two rupees change.

Turning our backs on Martoli and the mountains we marched down the valley towards the plains.

CHAPTER XIX

LAST DAYS

———◆———

THE SHORT, SWEET GRASS of the Martoli spur was soon left behind and the road grew ever rougher as the towering walls of the valley closed in upon the river, so that soon we were marching through a wild and savage gorge out of which we were not to escape until the second day. The gorge of the Gori, or 'white' river, rivals the Rishi gorge in its stark and gloomy grandeur and surpasses it in length and continuity. For twenty miles there is scarcely any break in the precipitous nature of either bank of the river, and in this distance the fall is about 4000 ft. The river runs with such violence and rapidity that for many miles it is nothing but a series of cascades and rapids. The rough track is nowhere level, climbing up and down, crossing and recrossing the river as it avoids impassable rock faces and seeks a way over the many torrents that come leaping down the sides of the great gorge. At one point, thinking we had already seen the last of snow for many a month, we were astonished to find ourselves walking over a huge avalanche cone of hard, dirty snow. Considering the time of the year and the altitude of only about 9000 ft., the presence of this snow is a convincing witness to the little sunlight that reaches the bottom of this deep and narrow cleft, and the depth of the winter snowfall.

There were no villages in the gorge, indeed no habitations of any kind, and at five o'clock, in pouring rain, we found shelter in a big cave. There were already five travellers and drovers in it who occupied the best pitch, and who did not invite us to join them round their fire. However, when Pasang asked them for some tea one of them gave us a handful of the stalks they use as tea and refused indignantly to take any of our sugar in exchange. At dusk six more wayfarers arrived and, finding the ground floor occupied, took possession of a second story reached by a difficult rock climb up a slab. We thought it was now time to put out a 'House Full' notice, but in this we were mistaken, for, after dark, five more men came in and found a niche for themselves in yet a third story.

When we woke to another wet morning most of the hotel guests had already left, apparently without any breakfast, and by half-past five we were left in sole possession and with a feeling that we were disgracefully late risers. We regretted this laziness because we had planned to touch some of our fellow lodgers for some atta, to make the chapatties for which our hearts yearned. We breakfasted austerely off satu.

All that morning the gorge continued to amaze us with its ruggedness and the road by its makers' ingenuity. It was carried backwards and forwards across the river on spidery bridges, it was carried up slabs on wooden stairs, across cliff faces on cunningly built stone revetments, and through tunnels carved out of solid rock. The gloominess and the severity of the scene, the rain and the eternal roar of the river, became oppressive, so that we were glad when the gorge at length opened out, and the track climbed up out of the valley to a gentler land of villages and fields.

We stopped at the village of Munsiari, where we were able to buy some flour and some rice, but we were worried about the state of our purse because we had only a few rupees, apart from a note for Rs 100, which was as valuable in these parts as waste paper. Even at this short distance from the mountains the peasants were as different from the frank, self-sufficient Bhotias of Martoli as chalk from cheese. We seemed to have nothing in common, and they displayed not the slightest interest or curiosity in us or our doings. And this, I think, without any implications of self-importance on our part, can only be attributed to the apathy of ignorance.

We were both by now terribly foot-sore and we learnt later that the rest of the party suffered in the same way. It may have been due to the cold and wet feet we frequently had on the mountain or to the wearing of several pairs of socks for a long period, and now that we had gone back to rubbers we felt like penitents condemned to walking in shoes full of peas or pebbles. In spite of this we sturdily refused to put on climbing boots again, even though this refusal meant an extra 5 lb. weight on our backs. Walking through hot valleys in heavy climbing boots is as incongruous as it is tiring, and for me it had become a point of honour to return to Ranikhet shod with the same rubbers in which I had started, although there was now little but the soles remaining.

Our loads, of which to relieve us we had not yet been able to hire a coolie, weighed us down and made us limp the more, but for all that it was difficult not to enjoy every minute of this march. The trees, the grass, the paddy fields, the birds; the streams in which we bathed and which, on one memorable occasion, provided us with a meal of fresh caught fish.

The streams were not always so friendly, for one of them nearly cost Houston his passage which we were racing to catch. At a place of evil memory called Tejam, we camped in a field of wheat-stubble by a big river called the Ramganga, and it is difficult to say which were the most trying, the villagers or a small venomous fly known locally as 'mora'. The villagers adopted what we found on this march to be their usual *non-possumus* attitude in the matter of food, but an ex-soldier of the Kumaon Rifles came to the rescue with some rice and milk. In all our travels in Garhwal it was always the reservist, usually of the Garhwal or the Kumaon Rifles, who was the most willing to help and the ablest. While talking to him we learnt the unexpected news that the bridge over the river was down—had been down in fact for two years. There did not appear to be the remotest chance of fording it, but he told us that two miles up there was a ford. To offset our relief he was careful to add that it was a difficult ford and that sometimes the water was up to a man's neck. Provided it did not rain in the night, he thought we might get across and volunteered to come with us to lend a hand. After paying him for the rice and milk we had only one rupee left, and, as we should have to travel for at least two more days before there was any hope of changing our Rs 100 note, we could not afford to pay him for any services rendered and had to decline his offer.

From the colour of the river, a lovely turquoise, we judged it not to be a glacier-fed stream, but in this we were mistaken, for we found later that it rises under the southern slopes of Nanda Kot. A heavy thunderstorm up the valley soon changed the colour to mud and we were concerned to hear the thunder growling away for most of the night. It was raining in the morning, and when we set off at seven it got steadily worse. The path was ill-defined, but having made what we thought was a liberal two miles we began to look for the ford.

The path appeared to terminate at the water's edge at a place where the river momentarily slackened the pace of its current, and on the far side we thought we could make out a continuation of the path. Much against our wishes we concluded that this must be the ford, but it looked so uninviting that, before trying it, we went a bit farther up stream. We could see no path, so we sent Pasang on to try higher up while Houston and I went back to what we now feared was the ford. Linking hands we took to the water, but had not covered more than a few yards out of the necessary fifty before we were up to our waists and hard put to it, even in this comparatively slack water, to keep our feet on the bottom. We turned back, convinced that there must be some mistake, for the water there would be up to a giraffe's neck let alone a man's.

While we were in the water we saw two men striding along the path who beckoned to us to come back. They were going to the ford they said and advised us to follow, and on they went again at a furious pace. They were active, long-legged beggars, with a minimum of clothing, and they carried a little bundle of short bamboo sticks, and clutched in one hand a great bamboo pole about 8 ft. long. I assumed this must be a necessary item of equipment for crossing the ford, and thought dismally how singularly ill-provided we were for pole-jumping with ice-axes 3 ft. long. However, there was not much time for thought as we had practically to run to keep them in sight; I imagined that they were as nervous as we were that the heavy rain, which still persisted, would make the river unfordable, possibly for several days.

We picked up Pasang, and a mile farther up they turned down towards the river and began removing the little surplus apparel they had preparatory to business. It was a curious place and the obvious one for a ford, for the river ran over a bed of shingle flats perhaps 300 yards wide. The water flowed in four separate channels, divided by banks of shingle, and the crossing of the first two of these was so easy as to make us think that it was all over bar shouting. The sight of the third soon dispelled this impression, and we watched with anxiety while our long-legged and half-naked friends tackled it. It was not very deep, just over the knees, but the speed of the current made one gasp. Their technique was instructive but quite impossible for us to emulate with the heavy loads we had. They took a diagonal line down stream,

not attempting to stem the current, and went as fast as they could, lift-
ing the foot clear of the water at every bound. In a few moments they
were safe on the far side, laughing at us as we advanced slowly and
fearfully into midstream hand in hand. The effort required to maintain
any footing was tremendous and it was difficult to keep the point of an
ice-axe on the bottom to support one. Houston cast off from us and
attempted to finish at speed, as they had done, but in the deepest part
he lost his footing and I thought he was gone, but after rolling right
over he struggled up again and reached the bank. Pasang and I were
still ten yards from the shore and making very heavy weather of it, so
I was mightily relieved when one of the bamboo merchants dashed
in and caught me by the hand. We were soon over the rest, and I was
so thankful to have the Ramganga behind us that I bestowed on our
deliverers nearly all the tobacco I had left.

    Travel in the Himalaya involves sooner or later the bridging or
fording of rivers, and it is surprising what can be crossed with an axe,
a few straight trees, and a good eye for a likely place for a bridge; and
when fording, how great is the assistance obtained from a rope, an ice-
axe, and the mutual support of two or more persons. In dangerous
rivers it is advisable to carry the load so that it can easily be slipped
off, for though a load helps to keep your feet on the bottom, once that
footing is lost the same load would be a fatal handicap.

    Two more days of hard going, getting daily more footsore, and
we reached Kapkot in the valley of the Sarju river on the route to the
Pindari glacier. This is a deservedly popular tourist route, well provided with dak bungalows, the last of which is but a mile or two from
the glacier snout. The one-horse village of Kapkot seemed in our eyes
a wealthy metropolis, for there were several native shops and a big dak
bungalow pleasantly situated on a green lawn above the river, and
shaded by an enormous banyan tree.

    The caretaker of the bungalow was not much impressed by our
appearance, and indeed if we were to be taken at our face value this was
quite understandable. Very grudgingly he opened one of the rooms for
us and began, metaphorically, to count his spoons; but when he asked
where our coolies were, and we were obliged to confess that the faith-
ful but dishevelled Pasang was the sole member of our suite, he seemed
half inclined to shut it again. We had no cash at all now except for the

Rs 100 note, and, large though Kapkot appeared to us, we doubted whether the combined population could find change for this amount. If this, as we expected, proved true, then our creditors would be asked to accompany us on the march until we were, as it were, solvent; nor did we allow this consideration to make us stint ourselves in the orders we gave to the caretaker for the provision of food. However, when we did produce the note as an earnest of good faith the eyes of the care-taker shone with a sudden geniality, and he hastened to assure us that change would be found. His former surliness was forgotten, he became profoundly respectful, and bustled about throwing open doors, set-ting chairs and tables, attending to our wants in every way he could.

Being now on the well-ordered Pindari glacier route it was from here on nothing but roses, roses, all the way. At the next halt Bageswar, the Rawal of the temple, a fine type of Indian gentleman of the old school, very dignified and erect in spite of his age, sent us with his customary generosity a present of fruit; a party who were also stopping at the bungalow pressed upon us a loaf of bread and an enormous fish out of the Sarju river, while the khansama in charge of the bungalow served up a four-course dinner. I had been this way before and had promised Houston that at Bageswar we would get a five-course dinner, but this disappointment he generously overlooked.

Bageswar is not the prosperous market town that it once was when its traders acted as middlemen between the Bhotias and the plainsmen. Now the Bhotias deal direct with the banias of Haldwani, Tanakpur, and Ramnagar at the foot of the hills. The bazaar consists of solid well-built houses with shops on the ground floor, but it was sad to see so many of these shut up.

There is a very old temple here; the present building, which is by no means the first, is said to date back to A.D. 1450. It is over this that our benefactor the Rawal, Poona Sahib, presides, a man who through-out a long life has stood for unswerving loyalty to the British Raj under very difficult circumstances.

At Someswar we joined the road from Ranikhet to Garul which we had travelled over in a bus on the way out, and all that remained for us now was to find some conveyance. The *deus ex machina* soon appeared in the guise of a native chauffeur who was, he said, waiting here for his master who had disappeared into the blue and had not returned. At least that was the tale that was told to us, but we asked no questions and, for a consideration, we were wafted into Ranikhet in a high-powered, opulent-looking, new car. A kindness Pasang returned by being sick all over the rich upholstery of the back seat.

We reached Ranikhet on September 12th and took up our quarters once more in the Forest Bungalow, where we found, to our sorrow, that the keen edge of our desires was already dulled by the good things we had found at Bageswar. Houston left on the 13th and I sat down alone to await the arrival of the main body, for there were porters to pay off and various matters to be settled.

The first to arrive came in on the 19th and the last, I think, on the 21st, on which day, by the way, Houston, who was flying, was already in Paris. And, for one night only, the party was reunited before another and final dispersal took place.

There were several lessons to be learnt from this show, but of too technical a nature to be discussed here. We live in an age of mechanisation and, in recent years, it has become apparent that even mountaineering is in danger of becoming mechanised. It is therefore pleasing to record that in climbing Nanda Devi no mechanical aids were used—apart that is from the apricot brandy. Our solitary oxygen apparatus was fortunately drowned, pitons were forgotten at the Base, snow shoes and crampons were solemnly carried up only to be abandoned, and I hope it is clear that the glacier drill with which we burdened ourselves was a scientific instrument and not a device for facilitating glacier travel.

Another interesting point is that the age limit for high climbing, previously put at 35, seems to have expanded, for our party was of all ages from twenty-two to over fifty, but I do not want to imply that either of these extremes is the best. Porters for high camps were found to be not indispensable, and a certain amount of hard work and hard living on the march up did not incapacitate anyone for work on the mountain. Even stranger was the fact that men of two different nations could work together under trying conditions in complete harmony and without jealousy.

It was but a short three months that we had met, many of us as strangers, but inspired by a single hope and bound by a common purpose. This purpose was only achieved by team-work, team-work the more remarkable on account of the two different nationalities; and though these two nations have a common origin they are for that reason more critical of each other's shortcomings—as relationship leads proverbially to ill-feeling. The Americans and ourselves do not always see eye to eye, but on those rare occasions when we come together to do a job of work, as, for example, in war or in the more serious matter of climbing a mountain, we seem to pull together very well.

Where each man pulled his weight each must share the credit; for, though it is natural for each man to have his own aspirations, it is in mountaineering, more than in most things, that we try to believe

> The game is more than the players of the game,
> And the ship is more than the crew.

H. W. TILMAN

The Collected Edition

FOR THE FIRST TIME SINCE THEIR ORIGINAL APPEARANCE, all fifteen books by H. W. Tilman are being published as single volumes, with all their original photographs, maps and charts. Forewords and afterwords by those who knew him, or who can bring their own experience and knowledge to bear, complement his own understated writing to give us a fuller picture of the man and his achievements. A sixteenth volume is the 1980 biography by J. R. L. Anderson, *High Mountains and Cold Seas*. The books will appear in pairs, one each from his climbing and sailing eras, in order of original publication, at quarterly intervals from September 2015:

Sep 2015	Snow on the Equator
	Mischief in Patagonia
Dec 2015	The Ascent of Nanda Devi
	Mischief Among the Penguins
Mar 2016	When Men and Mountains Meet
	Mischief in Greenland
Jun 2016	Mount Everest 1938
	Mostly Mischief
Sep 2016	Two Mountains and a River
	Mischief Goes South
Dec 2016	China to Chitral
	In Mischief's Wake
Mar 2017	Nepal Himalaya
	Ice With Everything
Jun 2017	Triumph and Tribulation
	High Mountains and Cold Seas

www.tilmanbooks.com